# THE ORIGAMI HOME

# THE ORIGAMI HOME

## MORE THAN 30 PROJECTS TO CRAFT, FOLD, AND CREATE

MARK BOLITHO

WITH PHOTOGRAPHY BY MICHAEL WICKS

RUNNING PRESS
PHILADELPHIA · LONDON

This book has been produced by Jacqui Small LLP,
An imprint of Aurum Press Ltd,
74–77 White Lion Street, London N1 9PF
Text and projects copyright © 2014 Mark Bolitho
Photography, design, and layout copyright
© 2014 Jacqui Small
The author's moral rights have been asserted.

First published in the United States in 2014 by
Running Press Book Publishers,
A Member of the Perseus Books Group

Books published by Running Press are available at
special discounts for bulk purchases in the United
States by corporations, institutions, and other
organizations. For more information, please contact
the Special Markets Department at the Perseus Books
Group, 2300 Chestnut Street, Suite 200, Philadelphia,
PA 19103, or call (800) 810-4145, ext. 5000, or e-mail
special.markets@perseusbooks.com.

ISBN 978-0-7624-5420-4
Library of Congress Control Number: 2014935895

E-book ISBN 978-0-7624-5564-5

9  8  7  6  5  4  3  2  1
Digit on the right indicates the number of this printing

All projects and designs in this book must
be reproduced only for personal use and
not for commercial purposes.

**Publisher:** Jacqui Small
**Associate Publisher:** Joanna Copestick
**Senior Editor:** Claire Chandler
**Senior Project Editor:** Zia Mattocks
**Art Director:** Sarah Rock
**Set Designer:** Paul Tilby
**Production:** Maeve Healy

Running Press Book Publishers
2300 Chestnut Street
Philadelphia, PA 19103-4371

Visit us on the web!
www.runningpress.com

MARK BOLITHO has been involved with origami for more than 30 years and is presently Chair of the British Origami Society. In 2004 he started working professionally on paper-folding projects, including undertaking commissions, product design, creating kits, and writing books on the subject.

Mark has worked on a wide range of projects, from conventional model-making for photography to large-scale displays for events and exhibitions. His work, which includes advertising campaigns, workshops, lectures, and demonstrations, has taken him around the world, from London, where he is based, to the United States, Canada, Dubai, Singapore, Japan, and Korea. He has also been a consultant on several projects where designers have used origami techniques in product development. Among his clients are Hewlett-Packard, Canon, BBC TV, Sony, and the Telegraph newspaper group. Mark is the author of several books about origami, including *Crease Lightning* (1998). www.creaselightning.co.uk

MICHAEL WICKS completed a degree in Fine Art, specializing in photography, before beginning a career as a professional photographer. His passion for his craft meant that he quickly established a name for himself with his ability to produce beautiful images across a wide range of subject matter. For more than 20 years he has worked in the studio and on location for publishers, architects, designers, and corporate clients, in addition to many of his own projects. His work has appeared in numerous publications, encompassing lifestyle, fashion, music, food, and art and craft. Michael also makes guitars and furniture in his spare time.

# CONTENTS

# INTRODUCTION

THE ORIGINS OF PAPER FOLDING are uncertain, although it is often attributed to Japan (hence the adoption of the Japanese term "origami"). There are records of Japanese paper folding in early prints, and the first known book of folding instructions—*Senbazaru Orikata* or *The Secrets of One Thousand Cranes Origami*—was published in Japan in 1797. However, there are also strong paper-folding traditions outside Japan. In Korea, for example, there are many traditional ceremonial paper folds, and in Europe there is a parallel tradition of fabric folding, where table coverings and napkins were folded for the banquets of noblemen. Over time, there was a transition between East and West, and it is thought that some of the early paper-folded models were shared with the West by traveling Oriental magicians demonstrating the flapping bird.

Whatever the origins, contemporary paper folding has come a long way from its traditional roots. The application of mathematics and experimentation with new techniques have led to the development of more complex forms, while advances in paper-making technology have led to the development of lighter, more malleable paper and, as a result, more complex models.

There is a long tradition of furniture models in paper folding, and there are many tables and chairs among the traditional models of Japan and

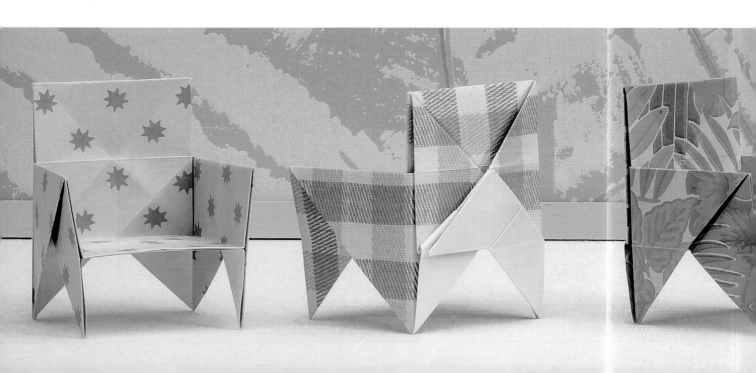

Korea. However, it is a genre that is often overlooked. This collection of paper-folded furniture has contemporary origins. It represents more than ten years of development of furniture designs and includes many unpublished projects. Some of the models were developed in response to commissions, while others were developed specifically for this book. The armchair on page 16 evolved from a project that required chairs for a paper office. Over time, the model was reused in various projects and expanded to become a sofa. Gradually the folding process was refined to the model shown here. Some of the other models have similar stories.

The book also considers another area of paper folding—the use of patterned and colored papers. The choice of paper is important, as it determines how the final model will look. The models can be made as stand-alone pieces or as part of a collection, with each element forming part of a colour coordinated room.

The folding process for each model is illustrated by a series of step-by-step instructions describing its construction. The "Getting Started" section explains the symbols used and gives some advice for following the instructions. If you are new to paper-folding, then start with the easy chair on page 12, which has been included as an introductory project.

Once you have mastered the models, experiment by making them in different patterns and designs. Work on coordinating colors and patterns across related projects and within overall room designs.

**BELOW** The armchair on page 93 is shown here made up in several different patterned papers, demonstrating how your choice of paper can dramatically alter the look of your finished model.

# GETTING STARTED

The folding process is explained with a series of step-by-step instructions leading to a finished model. Each step explains one or two folds and should be followed in order. When a step is completed, it should look like the image in the next step. If it doesn't, undo the folds and try again.

## ARROWS

The transition from one step to the next is explained by a series of lines and arrows that represent the folds required for each step. The lines indicate where the folds should be made, and the arrows indicate how the paper should be moved to make the folds (see right).

## FOLDS

All folds can be described as either a mountain fold or a valley fold. These names refer to how the surface of the paper will look after the fold has been applied. A mountain fold causes the paper to fold toward the observer, and a valley fold causes it to fold away. Each of the two folds is shown by a different line style (see right).

## SYMBOLS

Standard origami diagram notation includes various symbols that are used to explain the folding process, such as turning the model over, rotating it, or repeating a step (see below).

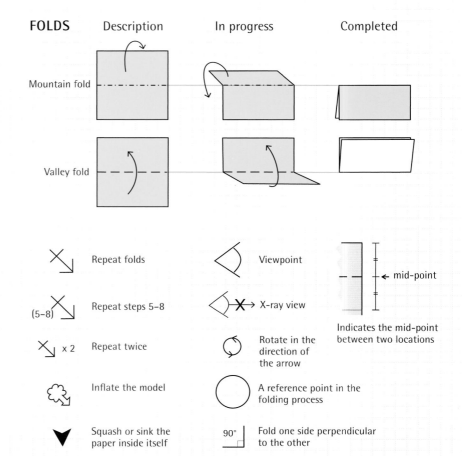

**ARROWS**

Fold

Fold and unfold

(2)     Fold over two layers

**FOLDS**    Description    In progress    Completed

Mountain fold

Valley fold

Repeat folds

(5–8)   Repeat steps 5–8

× 2   Repeat twice

Inflate the model

Squash or sink the paper inside itself

Viewpoint

X-ray view

Rotate in the direction of the arrow

A reference point in the folding process

90°   Fold one side perpendicular to the other

← mid-point

Indicates the mid-point between two locations

Cut the paper where indicated

The next step will show the model turned over top to bottom

The next step will show the model turned over left to right

# FOLLOWING INSTRUCTIONS

Follow the steps in number order. Before making the folds in any step, look ahead to see how the model should look when the folds have been applied. Then look at the current step and see how the process is described. Folds are often explained using reference points to enable accurate folding. When folding a model in half, match up the edges, make the fold, and then crease. Fold on a flat and level surface. The upper side of the paper or model is shown with a pattern or color and the underside is white.

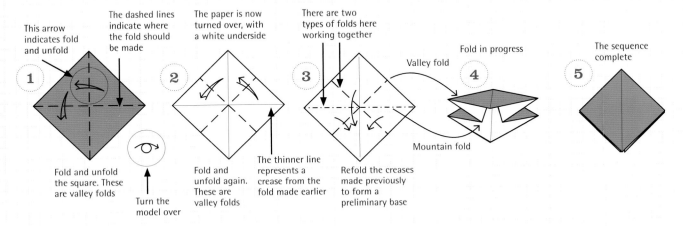

This arrow indicates fold and unfold

The dashed lines indicate where the fold should be made

The paper is now turned over, with a white underside

There are two types of folds here working together

Valley fold

Fold in progress

The sequence complete

Mountain fold

Fold and unfold the square. These are valley folds

Turn the model over

Fold and unfold again. These are valley folds

The thinner line represents a crease from the fold made earlier

Refold the creases made previously to form a preliminary base

# FOLDING SQUARES AND RECTANGLES

Models in the book are presented as groups of related objects as parts of a room set. Each project is accompanied by a recommended size of starting sheet—either a square or rectangle—that will make all of the objects proportional to one another. Choose a starting rectangle of the appropriate size from the pocket at the back of the book and cut to size. Alternatively, use your own choice of paper.

### SQUARES FROM RECTANGLES

The projects in this book are generally made from squares and regular rectangles. The following method shows how to make a square from a standard rectangle. A square has sides of equal length, so by folding the upper edge of a rectangle down it is possible to measure out a square with sides equal to the shorter side of the rectangle.

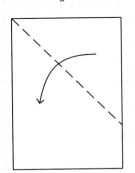

1 Fold the upper edge down to align with the opposite side.

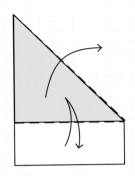

2 Fold and unfold the lower edge up and back down again along the folded-over edge.

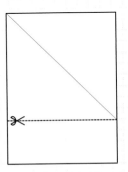

3 Cut along the crease and separate the two sections.

4 You now have a square and a residual rectangle.

## 2 X 1 RECTANGLES

The method for making a square can also be applied to make a 2 x 1 rectangle, which in turn can be made into a 3 x 2 rectangle.

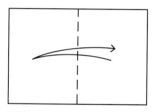 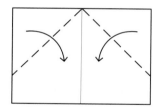 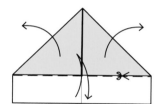 

1. Fold the rectangle in half and crease the middle line, then unfold.

2. Fold the outer corners into the middle crease.

3. Crease along the folded edges, then unfold the corners. Cut along the lower crease and separate the sections.

4. The upper section is a 2 x 1 rectangle.

## 3 X 2 RECTANGLES

1. Starting with a 2 x 1 rectangle, fold and unfold the right edge to the middle crease.

2. Cut along the crease and separate the two sections.

3. The resulting larger rectangle is proportioned 3:2.

4. The residual rectangle is proportioned 2:1.

## FOLDING A 6 X 4IN RECTANGLE (3:2)

The following method can be used to create a rectangular sheet of any size.

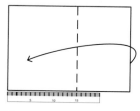 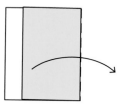 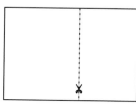  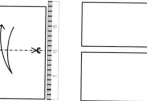

1. Use a ruler to measure a length of 6in along one axis. Fold the edge over at this point.

2. Align the edges of the paper. This will ensure that the crease line is perpendicular to the edge.

3. Cut along the crease.

4. Repeat this process on the opposite axis, making the fold and cutting the paper at the 4in mark.

5. You should now have a 6 x 4in rectangle.

# COLORS AND PATTERNS

THE CHOICE OF PAPER is an important aspect of paper folding. The color, texture, pattern, weight, and all of the composite qualities will dictate how the model folds and how the finished piece will look.

All of the models in the book can be made as stand-alone pieces, but they can also be made as related groups of furniture— a dining table and chairs, a bed and bedding, or a suite of furniture. Try experimenting with complementary colors and designs for a chosen group of objects.

The projects in this book are arranged in room sets, with each made up in a pattern or color that works as part of a coordinated scheme. However, although suggested, the patterns illustrated are not prescriptive and the projects can be made from any paper or pattern that you choose.

Suitable colored and patterned paper is available everywhere, but if you can't find the pattern you want, you can always design and print your own. The prototype projects for this book were made from wallpaper and giftwrap, and some of the early models for the workspace on page 82 were made from maps. Any paper that will hold a crease can be used for folding.

As you start to experiment with different papers, you will gain a better understanding of how a particular type of paper feels in your hands and how it will fold. The composition of the paper will determine how sharp the creases are. Once again, it is an aesthetic choice as to how your want the final model to look, and perhaps you would rather explore a softer effect for some of the pieces.

The furniture models can be combined in different ways. Just as in a real house, the chairs, tables, and lights can be moved around between rooms, and made in colors and patterns of your choice to create bespoke room sets to suit your own design aesthetic.

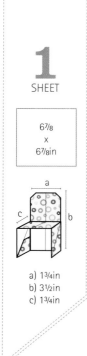

6⅞
x
6⅞in

a
c b

a) 1¾in
b) 3½in
c) 1¾in

# EASY CHAIR

This introductory model shows how a chair can be made from a minimal number of folds. Each step illustrates either mountain or valley folds until step 9, where both types are combined in a single procedure.

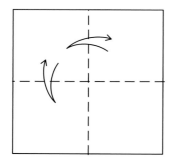

**1** Start with a square, colored side down. Fold and unfold it in half lengthwise along both axes.

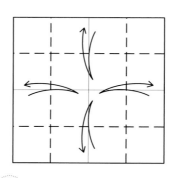

**2** Fold and unfold all four edges to the middle.

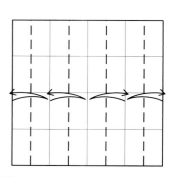

**3** Fold and unfold between the creases made previously.

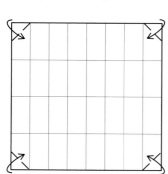

**4** Fold the corners in to the adjacent crease lines.

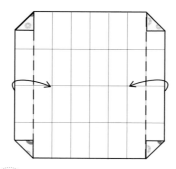

**5** Fold in the sides along the one-eighth crease lines.

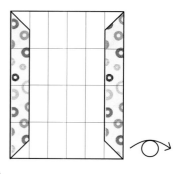

**6** Turn the model over (note the symbol).

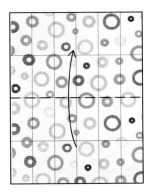

**7** Fold the lower edge up to touch the upper edge.

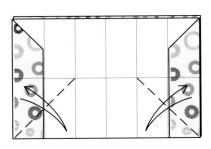

**8** Fold and unfold the upper layer diagonally between the outer corners and the second crease lines on both sides.

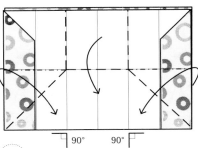

**9** Fold the outer edges in. This will cause the forward section to stand perpendicular to the back of the model, making it three-dimensional.

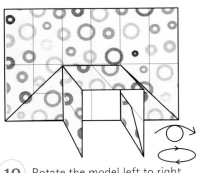

**10** Rotate the model left to right to work on the reverse.

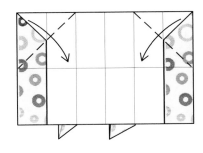

**11** Fold the upper corners in to the second crease lines on both sides.

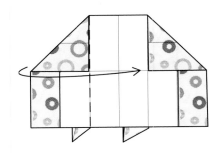

**12** Fold the left side in.

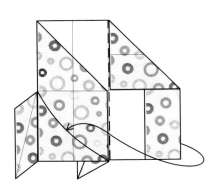

**13** Fold the right side over and tuck the lower corner into the pocket on the left side.

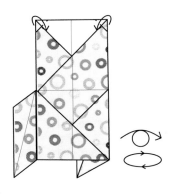

**14** Fold the upper corners over to shape the back, then turn the model over, left to right.

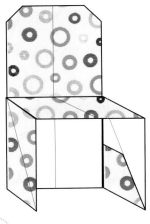

**15** Complete.

# LIVING ROOM

The living room is a space for relaxing and socializing, so this room has been designed for comfort and social interaction. The focal points are the coffee table and television, with the seating arranged around them. The main suite, comprising armchairs and a sofa, has thick, comfortable cushions forming the back and arm supports. A few coordinating throw pillows add to the relaxing mood. The patterns used for the furniture have been chosen to work with the wallpaper to enhance the calming atmosphere. Try experimenting with matching and contrasting colors to build a relaxing, contemporary living space.

**WALLS** Jane Churchill, Willowbrook, Red/Blue
**FLOOR** Little Greene, Heath Stripe, Cookie

6⅞
x
13¾in

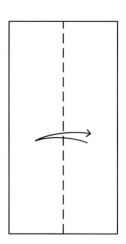

a) 2¾in
b) 2¾in
c) 2¾in

# CUSHIONED ARMCHAIR

The model design is based on making box shapes for the padding on the arms and the back of the chair. These box shapes create the look of substantial cushions and add to the character of a comfortable armchair. Try experimenting by curving the seat to give it a rounder, more lived-in look. The early steps of this model involve a lot of precreasing.

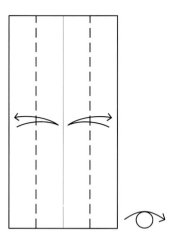

**1** Start with a 2 x 1 rectangle, colored side down. Fold and unfold the rectangle in half lengthwise.

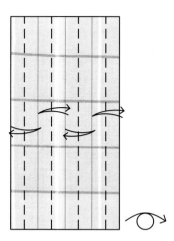

**2** Fold and unfold the rectangle between the sides and the middle crease. Then turn the model over.

**3** Fold and unfold between the creases made previously. Then turn the model over.

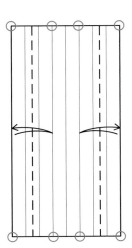

**4** Fold and unfold between the creases made previously.

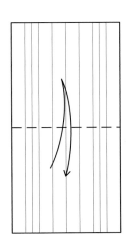

**5** Fold and unfold widthwise along the middle.

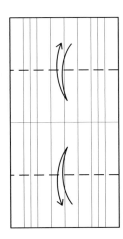

**6** Fold and unfold between the upper and lower edges and the middle crease.

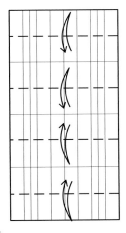

**7** Fold and unfold between the creases made previously.

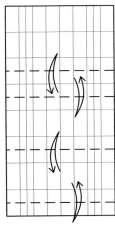

**8** Fold and unfold between the creases made previously.

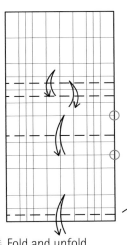

**9** Fold and unfold between the creases made previously. Then turn the model over.

**10** Fold the lower edge up where indicated.

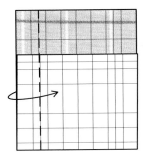

**11** Fold the left edge over.

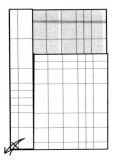

**12** Fold and unfold the bottom left folded edge.

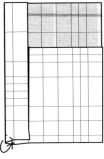

**13** Reverse-fold the corner into the folded edge.

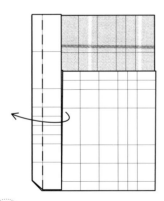

**14** Fold the edge back along the crease.

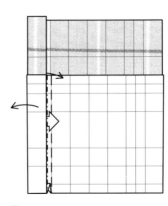

**15** Separate the layers of the paper trapped in the crease and turn one layer inside out.

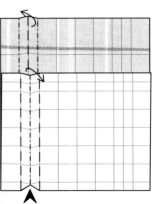

**16** Reverse out the paper. Separate the layers, reverse-fold in the triangle at the base, and flatten.

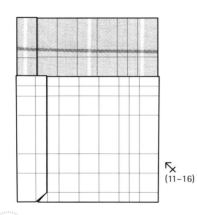

×
(11–16)

**17** Repeat steps 11–16 on the right side.

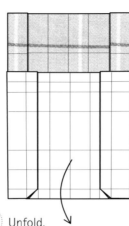

**18** Unfold.

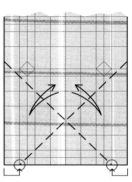

Lower section

**19** Fold and unfold diagonally where indicated. The folds should start from the first crease in. Note this when expanding the armchair to a sofa.

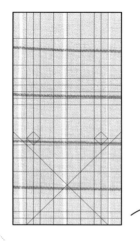

**20** Turn the model over.

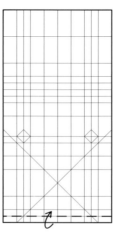

**21** Fold the lower edge up.

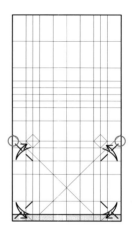

**22** Fold and unfold diagonally where indicated. Note the location of the reference crease highlighted by the red circles.

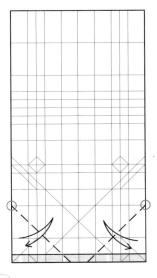

**23** Fold and unfold the lower corners diagonally where indicated. Note the origin of the crease on either side. Again, this is important for making the sofa.

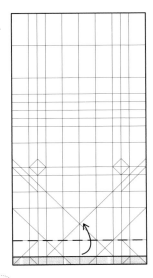

**24** Fold the lower edge up.

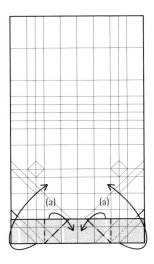

**25** Fold the folded edge in at (a). At the same time, fold over the corners along the creases made in step 23.

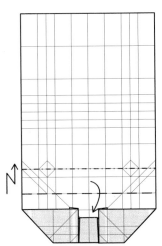

**26** Fold the upper section down and up again along the creases indicated.

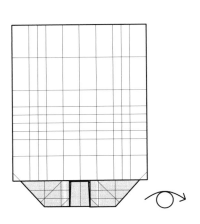

**27** Turn the model over.

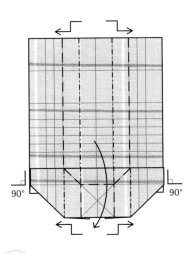

**28** Fold the edges in and out again, forming a raised section in the middle. At the same time, fold the upper section in to be perpendicular to the lower section.

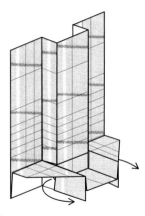

**29** Fold out the paper on both sides.

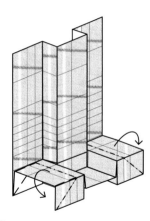

**30** Fold the edges of the paper down along diagonal folds on either side.

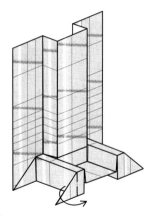

**31** Fold the left triangular point around to the front.

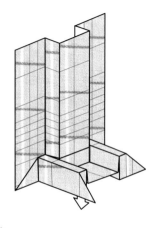

**32** Fold out the paper inside the triangular point.

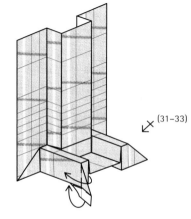

(31–33)

**33** Fold the triangular point back and tuck the edge of the paper underneath the adjacent folded edge to hold it in place. Repeat steps 31–33 on the other side.

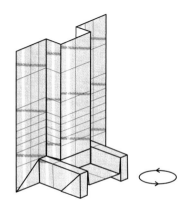

**34** Rotate the model to look at the reverse.

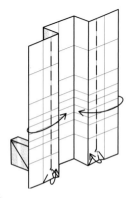

**35** Fold in the edges and reverse-fold the lower triangles up along the creases made in step 13.

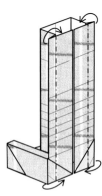

**36** Fold in the edges on both sides along the creases made in step 16. This will narrow the edges of the upper section compared to the arms.

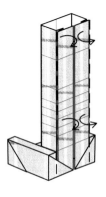

**37** Fold the edges out perpendicular to the model.

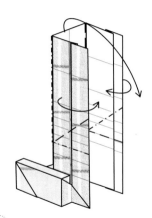

**38** Fold the upper section down to be perpendicular to the lower section. At the same time, fold the edges of the folded section in.

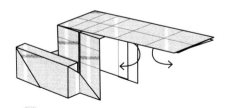

**39** Fold the edges out again.

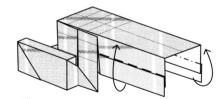

**40** Fold the edges up on both sides.

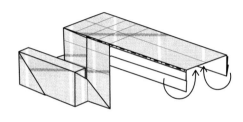

**41** Fold the edges up again to lie flat.

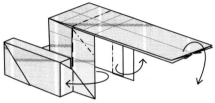

**42** Fold the upper section down and fold out the two sides.

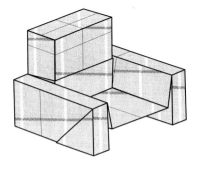

**43** Fold the outer edges in to the pockets formed by the edges of the folded section.

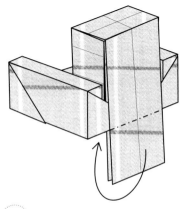

**44** Fold the lower edge of the section behind and into the model.

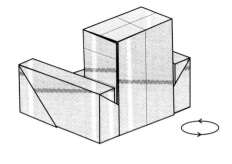

**45** Rotate the model.

**46** Complete.

8³/₄
x
13³/₄in

a) 4¹/₂in
b) 2³/₄in
c) 2³/₄in

# TWO-SEATER SOFA

The sofa is an evolution from the armchair on page 16, with the arms and back in the same style. The same folding process for making the arms is applied to the edges of a wider rectangle; the extra width makes a wider seat. Steps 1 to 8 show how to prepare the edges in advance of folding the arms from step 8 on page 17.

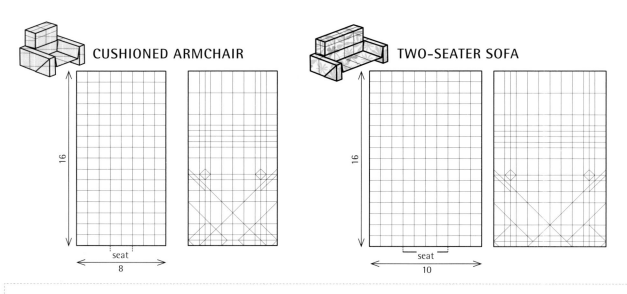

CUSHIONED ARMCHAIR

16

seat
8

TWO-SEATER SOFA

16

seat
10

**ARMCHAIR TO SOFA** The folding method used for the armchair can be applied to make a sofa. Maintaining the length of the starting rectangle will ensure that the sofa and armchair will be the same height; increasing the width will produce a wider seat. The armchair is made from an 8 x 16 rectangle; the two-seater sofa from a 10 x 16 rectangle.

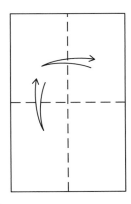

**1** Start with a 10 x 16 rectangle, colored side down. Fold and unfold the rectangle in half lengthwise.

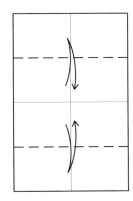

**2** Fold and unfold the upper and lower edges to the middle.

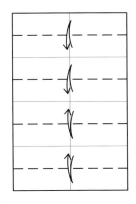

**3** Fold and unfold between the creases made previously.

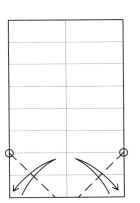

**4** Fold and unfold both of the lower corners up to the quarter crease.

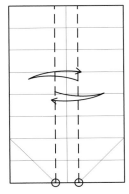

**5** Fold and unfold lengthwise at the points where the diagonal folds cut into the lower edge.

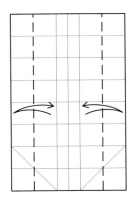

**6** Fold and unfold between the creases made previously.

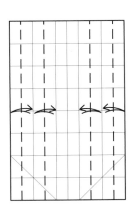

**7** Fold and unfold between the creases made previously.

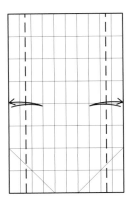

**8** Fold and unfold between the creases indicated. Then apply the folding sequence of the armchair from step 8 on page 17.

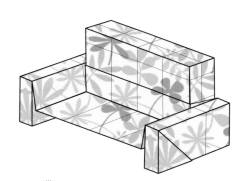

**9** Complete.

**1**
SHEET

3⁷⁄₁₆
x
3⁷⁄₁₆in

a
b

a) 1⅛in
b) 1⅛in

# THROW PILLOW

The throw pillow is made by folding a square into three along both axes, and then folding in the edges to make a windmill shape. The method for dividing the square into three is used in a few other projects, such as the bedcover and bedside table on pages 103 and 105, and is referred back to.

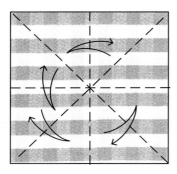

**1** Start with a square, colored side up. Fold and unfold it lengthwise and diagonally along both axes.

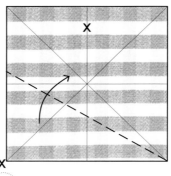

**2** Fold the lower left corner up. The fold should start from the right corner and cause the corner (x) to touch the center crease (x).

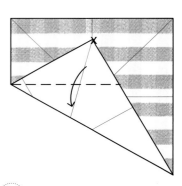

**3** Fold the corner down to touch the folded edge beneath.

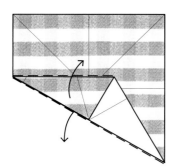

**4** Unfold back to a square.

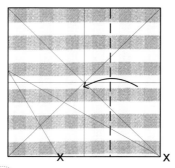

**5** Fold the right edge in, causing the corner (x) to touch the crease made in step 3.

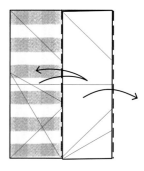

**6** Fold and unfold the opposite edge over, and open it back to a square.

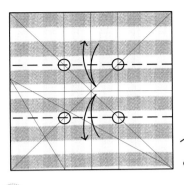

**7** Fold and unfold along the opposite axis, dividing the square into three sections. Turn the model over.

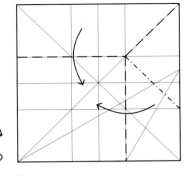

**8** Fold the upper and right edges in.

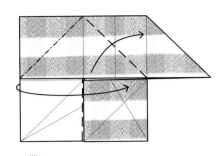

**9** Fold the upper layer up and the left side in.

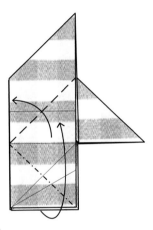

**10** Fold the lower section up and diagonally to the left.

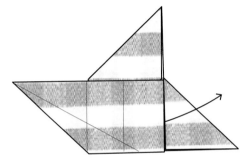

**11** Reverse out the paper trapped beneath.

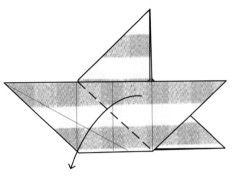

**12** Fold the upper right layer down along the diagonal to make a windmill shape.

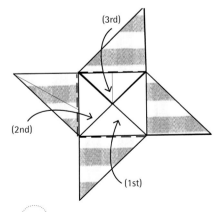

**13** Fold the corners in along the adjacent folded edge, working in order from 1st to 3rd.

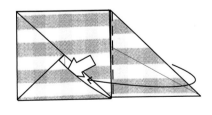

**14** Fold the last corner in and tuck it into the adjacent pocket made by the 1st folded corner.

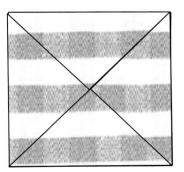

**15** Complete.

6⁵/₁₆
x
6⁵/₁₆in

a) 3¹/₈in
b) 3¹/₈in
c) 1³/₈in

# COFFEE TABLE

The geometry of a square lends itself perfectly to creating a table shape, and the corners are folded to form the legs. The method for folding the legs locks the inner section of the table together and makes the model more rigid.

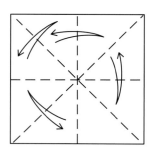

**1** Start with a square, colored side down. Fold and unfold the square in half lengthwise and diagonally.

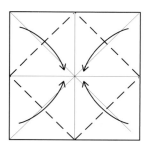

**2** Fold the corners to the middle.

**3** Fold the corners to the middle again, then unfold.

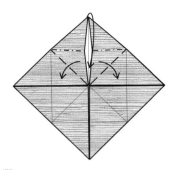

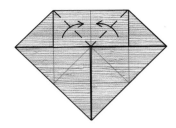

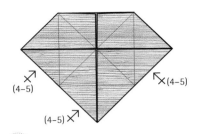

4. Fold the top corner down and open out the edges of the upper point.

5. Fold the corners up.

6. Repeat steps 4–5 on the other corners.

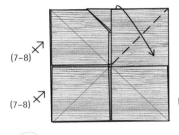

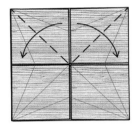

7. Fold one corner up. At the same time, reverse-fold the upper layer and flatten.

8. Fold the corner back. Then repeat steps 7–8 on the other corners.

9. Fold the upper corners down to open the upper edge.

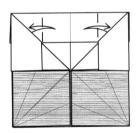

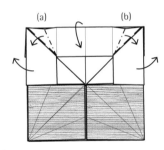

10. Fold the edge up. This will open up the paper in the layer beneath.

11. Fold and unfold the edges where indicated.

12. Fold the edges in, causing diagonal folds at (a) and (b).

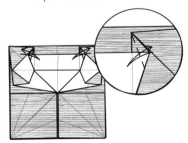

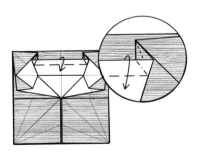

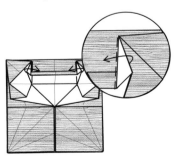

13. Fold and unfold the corners of the folded edge.

14. Fold the edge over, causing the previously folded edges to fold in.

15. Fold the corners back over.

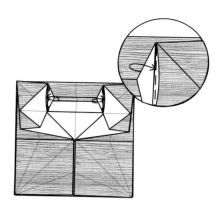
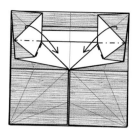

**16** Fold the corners over and tuck them into the layers of the adjacent folded edge.

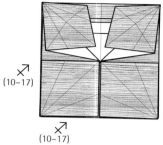

**17** Fold the upper layers back.

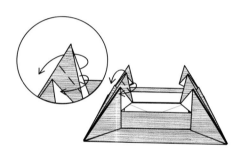

(10–17)

(10–17)

(10–17)

**18** Repeat steps 10–17 on the other edges.

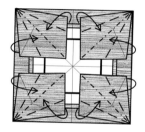

**19** On each of the four sections, fold the edges in and reverse the middle upward (see step 7).

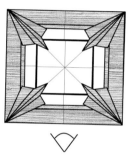

**20** Rotate the model to look at it from the side.

**21** Reverse-fold the tip of the folded leg to lock the paper together.

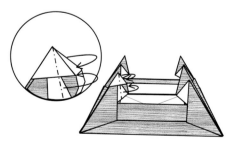

**22** Fold the inside edge of the leg behind and into the model.

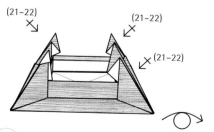

(21–22)

(21–22)

(21–22)

**23** Repeat steps 21–22 on the other legs. Then turn the model over.

**24** Complete.

# TELEVISION

SHEET

Television
6⁷/₈ x 6⁷/₈in

Computer Screen
6⁵/₁₆ x 6⁵/₁₆in

Television
a) 3in
b) 2in
c) ³/₄in

Computer Screen
a) 2³/₄in
b) 1⁷/₈in
c) ³/₄in

This model is designed around the main characteristic of a television, the screen. Having formed a screen shape, the paper is folded around it and the edges are tucked into one another to lock the model together, forming a simple television shape. The model can be used as a freestanding or wall-mounted television (see page 63) or as a screen for a computer (see page 85).

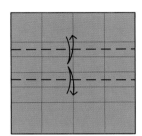

**1** Start with a square, colored side up. Fold and unfold the square in half lengthwise along both axes.

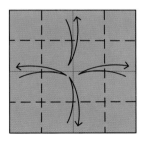

**2** Fold and unfold between the edges and the middle creases.

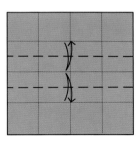

**3** Fold and unfold between the horizontal creases made previously.

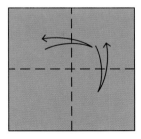

**4** Fold and unfold between the creases made previously.

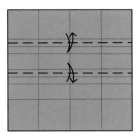

**5** Fold and unfold between the creases made previously.

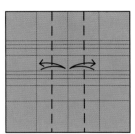

**6** Fold and unfold between the vertical creases made previously.

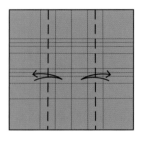

**7** Fold and unfold again between the creases made previously.

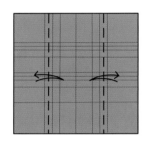

**8** Fold and unfold again between the creases made previously.

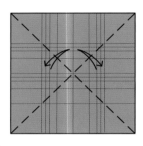

**9** Fold and unfold diagonally along both axes.

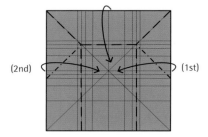

(2nd)          (1st)

**10** Fold in the sides and upper edge together along the folds indicated.

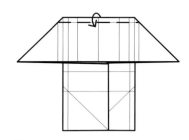

**11** Fold the upper edge down.

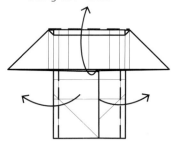

**12** Fold the edges out again along the creases indicated.

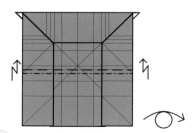

**13** Fold the lower edge up and down again as indicated. Then turn the model over.

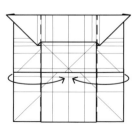

**14** Fold the sides in.

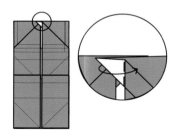

**15** Fold the tip of the corner over.

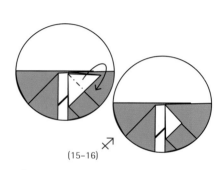

(15–16)

**16** Fold the tip of the corner behind. Repeat steps 15–16 on the other side.

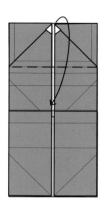

**17** Fold the upper section down.

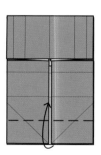

**18** Fold the lower section up to the crease indicated.

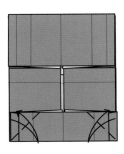

**19** Fold and unfold the corners of the lower section.

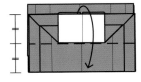

**20** Fold the upper layer of the lower section down. This will cause the edges to fold in.

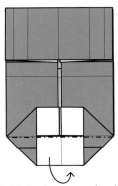

**21** Fold the lower section behind.

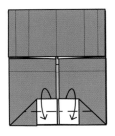

**22** Fold the edges down.

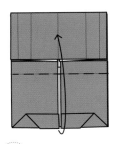

**23** Fold the lower section up.

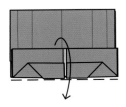

**24** Fold the upper edge of the section down again.

**25** Fold the whole section down.

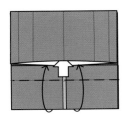

**26** Fold the lower section up and tuck it into the pocket in the upper section above.

For the TV stand, follow the instructions for the bench on page 70, using a 6⁷/₈ x 6⁷/₈ in square.

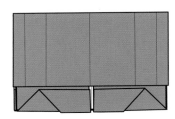

**27** Turn the model over.

**28** Complete.

**2**
SHEETS

Standard
Lamp Stand
3⁷⁄₁₆ x
6⁷⁄₈in

Lamp Shade
6⁷⁄₈ x
3⁷⁄₁₆in

Bedside
Lamp Base
2¹⁵⁄₁₆ x
2¹⁵⁄₁₆in

Lamp Shade
4⁵⁄₁₆ x
2³⁄₁₆in

Standard Lamp
a) 5¼in
b) 1¾in
c) 1¾in

Bedside Lamp
a) 1⅛in
b) 1⅜in
c) 1⅛in

# STANDARD LAMP

This is a two-piece model: one for the lamp stand, and the other for the shade. The height of the lamp can be changed by using a longer or shorter starting rectangle for the stand. A shorter stand can be used to create a table or bedside lamp (see page 107). Experiment by making lamp shades in different colors and shapes.

**LAMP STAND**

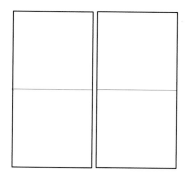

**1** Two equal 2 x 1 rectangles can be made by cutting a square in half.

**2** Start with a 2 x 1 rectangle, colored side down. Fold and unfold it along both axes to create the middle creases.

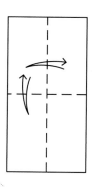

**3** Fold and unfold lengthwise between the edges and the middle creases. Then turn the paper over.

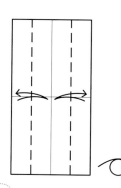

**4** Fold and unfold between the creases made previously.

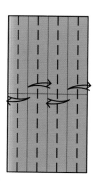

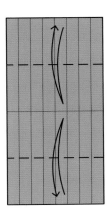 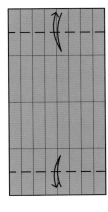 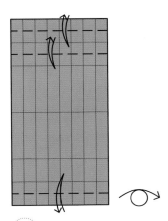

**5** Fold and unfold between the upper and lower edges and the middle.

**6** Fold and unfold between the creases made previously.

**7** Fold and unfold between the creases made previously. Turn the paper over.

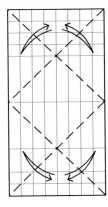 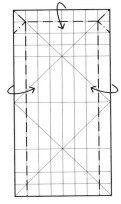 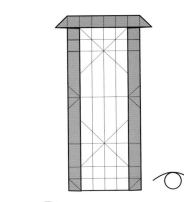

**8** Fold and unfold the outer corners diagonally.

**9** Fold the edges in on three sides along the creases made previously.

**10** Turn the model over.

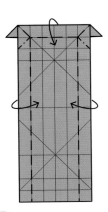 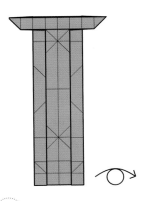 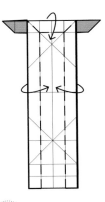 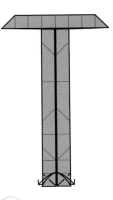

**11** Fold the sides and upper edge in along the creases made previously.

**12** Turn the model over.

**13** Fold the sides and upper edge in along the creases made previously.

**14** Fold and unfold the corners of the point.

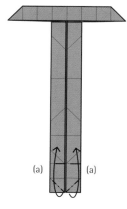

**15** Fold up the front layer of the two sides of the lower section, open out the layers beneath, and flatten.

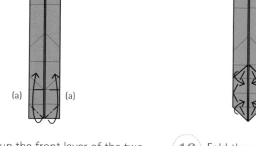

**16** Fold the corners in.

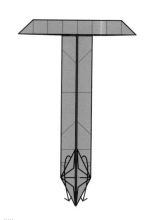

**17** Fold the points down.

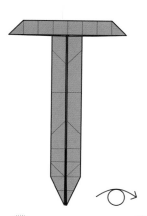

**18** Turn the model over.

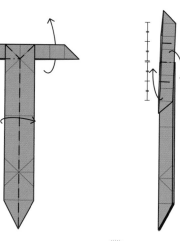

**19** Fold the model in half lengthwise. This will cause the upper T section to rotate and align with the lower section.

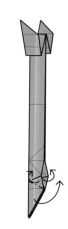

**20** Fold the upper section down and up again.

**21** Hold the lower corner and slide it up, folding the edges over the section above.

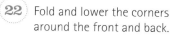

**22** Fold and lower the corners around the front and back.

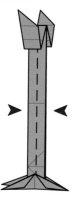

**23** Pinch the longer section, folding it in half and narrowing the stand.

**24** Stand complete.

# LAMP SHADE

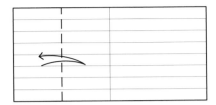 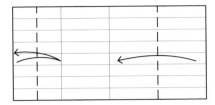 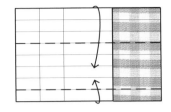

1. Start with a 2 x 1 rectangle, colored side down. Fold it into eight horizontal sections. Fold and unfold the left edge to the middle.

2. Fold and unfold the left edge to the crease made previously. Then fold the right edge to the adjacent crease.

3. Fold the upper and lower edges in where indicated.

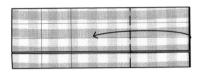 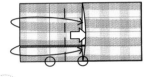 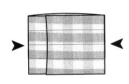 

4. Fold the right side over, along the edge of the folded side beneath.

5. Fold the left side over and tuck it into the other side.

6. Push the sides in and make a cylinder.

7. Lamp shade complete.

# PUTTING THE LAMP STAND AND SHADE TOGETHER

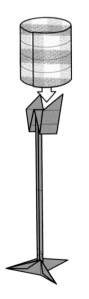 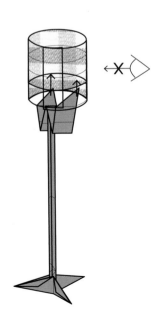 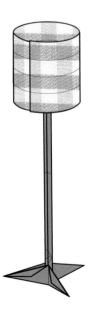

1. Insert the stand into the base of the lamp shade.

2. Tuck the corners beneath the folded edge inside the shade.

3. Complete.

# MODERN-
# RETRO
# DINING
# ROOM

This simple dining room set-up of four chairs around an octagonal table is presented in a mid-century modern style. The bright orange and yellow chairs are minimal, in keeping with the mid-century design ethos that placed great importance on functionality. The bold colors make them stand out and add impact to the room. The table is more subdued, but still vibrant with its striking gray-and-yellow geometric pattern. The table and chair are both fun to fold. Try experimenting with the layout by extending the table (see page 66) and adding more chairs to prepare for a banquet.

**WALLS** Mini Moderns, Festival Wallpaper, Concrete
**FLOOR** Mini Moderns, Darjeeling Wallpaper, Welsh Slate

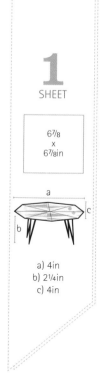

6⁷⁄₈
x
6⁷⁄₈in

a) 4in
b) 2¼in
c) 4in

# OCTAGONAL DINING TABLE

This table forms legs with diagonal folds at each corner (in contrast to the coffee table on page 26). Repeating the systematic leg-folding process on each corner will produce an octagonal table top, with the pattern in the middle of the starting square in the center. The corners of the octagon can be folded down to produce a square table top.

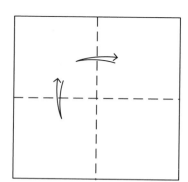

1  Start with a square, colored side down. Fold and unfold it in half lengthwise along both axes.

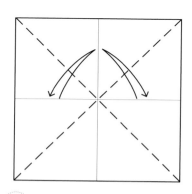

2  Fold and unfold the square in half diagonally along both axes.

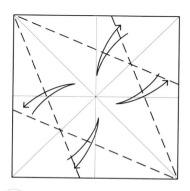

3  Fold and unfold the edges to the diagonal middle crease on both sides.

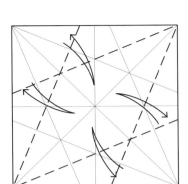

**4** Fold and unfold the edges to the middle crease on the other corners.

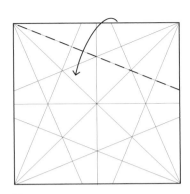

**5** Fold the upper edge down to the diagonal crease.

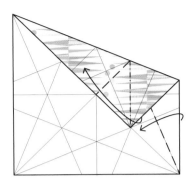

**6** Fold the right side in along the crease made previously. At the same time, fold the corner up and to the left.

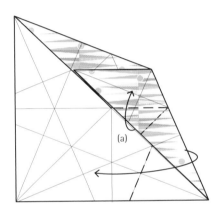

**7** Fold the edge up at (a). This will cause the lower right side to fold in along the crease made previously.

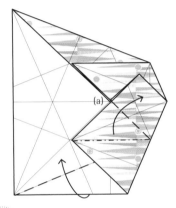

**8** Fold the corner over at (a). This will cause the lower edge to fold up.

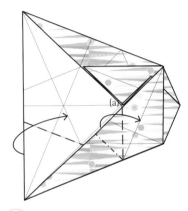

**9** Fold the middle of the folded edge over (a). This will cause the lower edge to fold up.

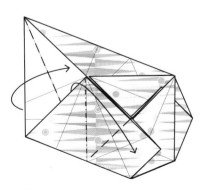

**10** Fold the corner over again. Continue to fold the outer edge in.

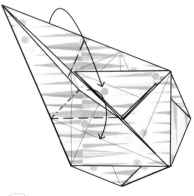

**11** Fold the middle of the edge over and fold the final section of the outer edge in.

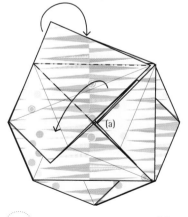

**12** Fold the corner over at (a). This will cause the outer edge to fold in.

**13** Fold the trapped corner over.

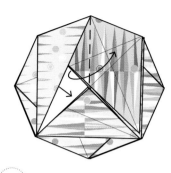

**14** Fold out the trapped paper. The folded section should look like the other three sections.

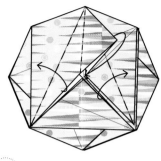

**15** Fold the edges of the folded corners out. This will cause the middle section to open. Fold it flat.

**16** Fold the left corner to the right.

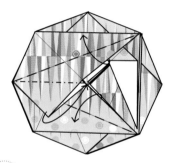

**17** Open out the edges of the corners and repeat the fold from step 15.

**18** Fold the corners over to reveal the next corner section.

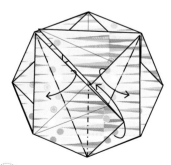

**19** Repeat step 15. Fold out the edges of the corners and flatten the middle section.

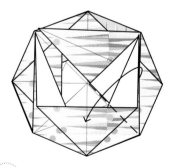

**20** Fold the corners back again.

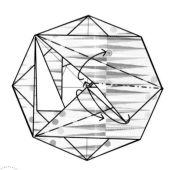

**21** Fold the edges out and flatten the folded corner on the final section.

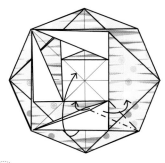

**22** Fold one of the points up, perpendicular to the base. Separate the layers and flatten the point.

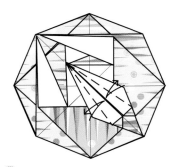

**23** Fold and unfold the edges of the squashed point to the middle.

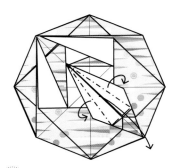

**24** Fold the point out again, folding the edges behind and reversing the folds made in step 23.

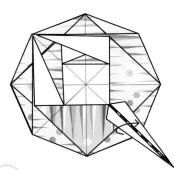

**25** Fold the point in half.

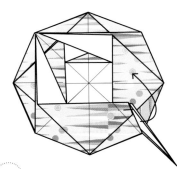

**26** Reverse-fold the point where indicated.

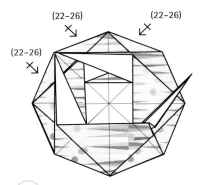

**27** Repeat steps 22–26 on the other three points.

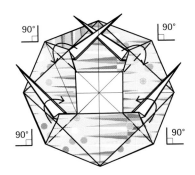

**28** Fold the points up to be perpendicular to the central section of the model.

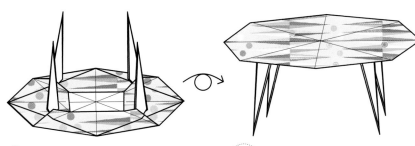

**29** Turn the model over and stand the table up.

**30** Complete.

**1**
SHEET

6⁵⁄₁₆
x
6⁵⁄₁₆in

a

b

c

a) 1⁵⁄₈in
b) 3¼in
c) 1⁵⁄₈in

# CLASSIC DINING CHAIR

A classic, clean-lined, four-legged chair, with legs
formed from the corners of a square. You could make four
chairs all in the same color or pattern, or create a mix-and-
match set to coordinate with your choice of dining
table pattern and set décor.

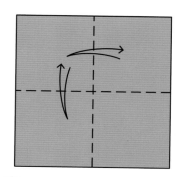

1 Start with a square, colored
side up. Fold and unfold it
in half lengthwise along
both axes.

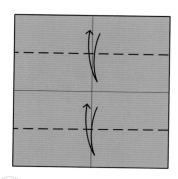

2 Fold and unfold the upper
and lower edges to the
middle crease.

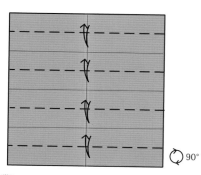

3 Fold and unfold between the
creases, dividing the square
into eight sections. Then
rotate the square 90°.

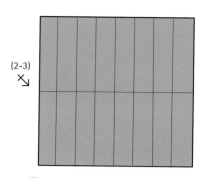

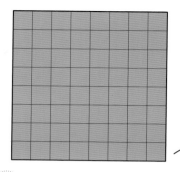

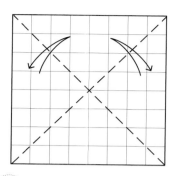

**4** Repeat steps 2–3 on the other axis.

**5** Turn the model over.

**6** Fold and unfold the square diagonally along both axes.

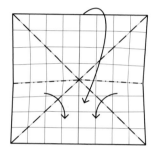

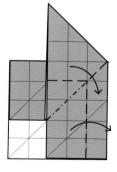

Fold in progress. This is sometimes called a waterbomb base.

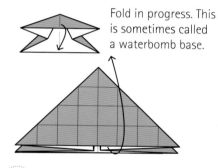

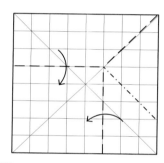

**7** Fold the upper edge down. At the same time, reverse-fold in the edges along the diagonal creases made in step 6.

**8** Open up the model.

**9** Fold the upper and right edges in simultaneously where indicated.

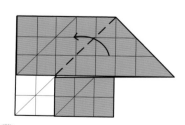

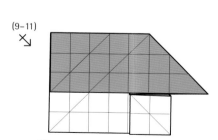

**10** Fold the right corner up.

**11** Fold the corner back and, at the same time, fold out the edge along the crease made previously.

**12** Repeat steps 9–11 on the other side.

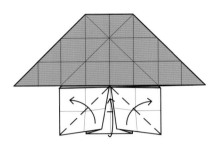

**13** Fold the inner edges of the lower section up diagonally. This will cause the lower edge to fold up.

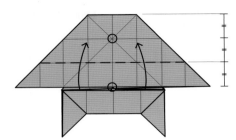

**14** Fold up the edge of the middle section one-third of the way up, and open and squash the paper in the layer beneath.

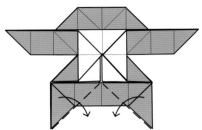

**15** Fold the lower corners down.

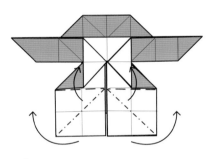

**16** Fold the lower sections up, causing two diagonal folds in the paper below. This will make two triangular points.

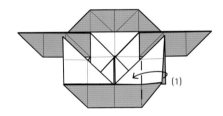

**17** Fold the upper layer over, causing the triangular point to open out.

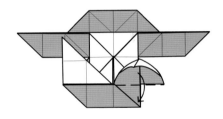

**18** Fold the section down.

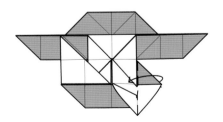

**19** Turn the section inside out and flatten the paper.

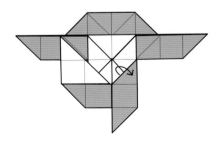

**20** Fold the paper in the layer beneath to the top.

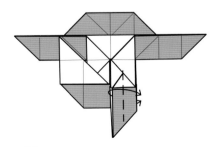

**21** Turn the point inside out by folding over the front and back layers simultaneously.

CLASSIC DINING CHAIR    45

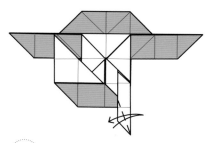

**22** Fold and unfold the lower edge of the point.

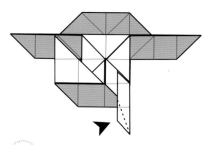

**23** Reverse the corner into the point.

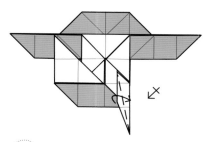

**24** Fold the edge over, on both the front and back, folding the leg in half.

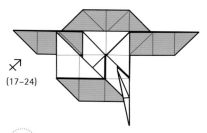

(17–24)

**25** Repeat steps 17–24 on the other side.

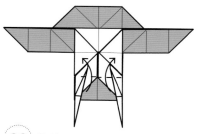

**26** Fold the points up.

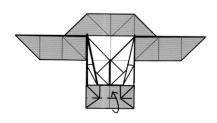

**27** Fold the lower edge up.

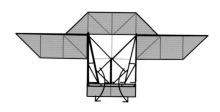

**28** Fold the legs back down again.

**29** Fold the edge of the upper section down.

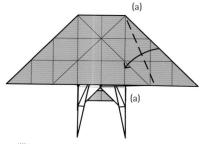

**30** Fold and unfold the right corner. The outer edge should touch the vertical crease (a)–(a).

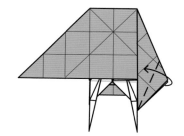

**31** Fold the lower right corner in. The outer edge should touch the adjacent folded edge.

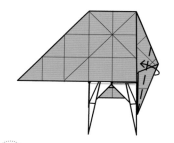

**32** Fold the edge in again.

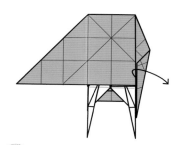

**33** Unfold the point back to step 30.

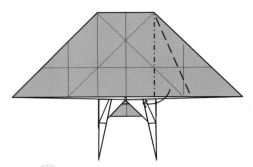

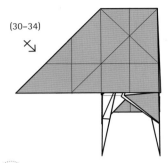

(30–34)

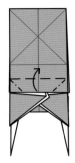

**34** Reverse-fold the corner into the model along the creases made previously.

**35** Repeat steps 30–34 on the other side.

**36** Fold the lower edge up to the crease above. The outer corners will fold in.

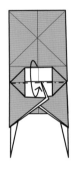

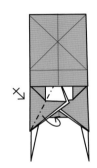

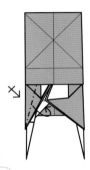

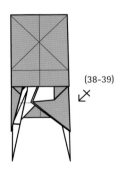

(38–39)

**37** Fold the edge down and reverse it inside the model.

**38** Fold the front and back edges of the trapped point inside, narrowing the leg.

**39** Fold the edges in again to narrow the point.

**40** Repeat steps 38–39 on the other leg.

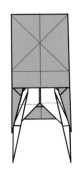

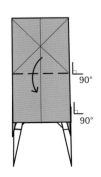

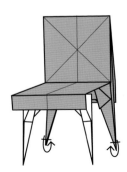

**41** Turn the model over, left to right.

**42** Fold the legs of the chair down and then fold the back of the chair forward.

**43** Fold the tips of the rear legs in to shorten them. This adjustment should make all four legs the same length and enable the chair to stand.

**44** Complete.

# PICTURE FRAME

**1**
SHEET

3 15/16
x
5 7/8 in

a

b

a) 4 5/16 in
b) 2 3/8 in

The picture frame is made by folding in the edge around a rectangular shape, in a similar technique to the television screen on page 29. Insert your chosen image at step 10, before the model is sealed. The picture can either be trimmed to size, or a frame can be made to fit around a selected image.

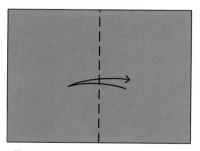

**1** Start with a rectangle, colored side up. Fold and unfold it in half widthwise.

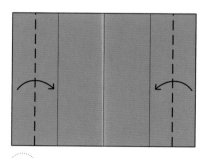

**2** Fold and unfold both sides to the middle.

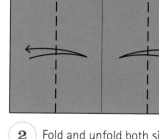

**3** Fold and unfold both sides to the creases made previously.

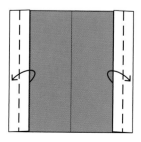

**4** Fold the inner edges out to the outer folded edges.

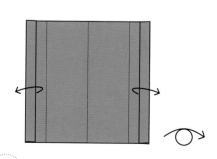

**5** Open it out back to a rectangle. Then turn it over.

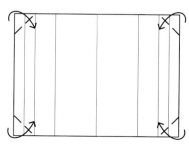

**6** Fold the corners in over the creases made previously.

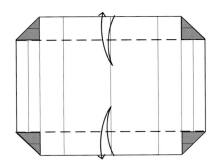

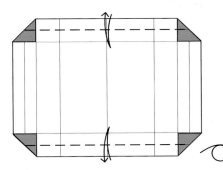

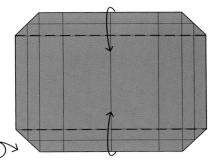

**7** Fold and unfold the upper and lower edges in along the edges of the folded triangles.

**8** Fold and unfold the upper and lower edges to the adjacent crease. Then turn the model over.

**9** Fold the upper and lower edges in.

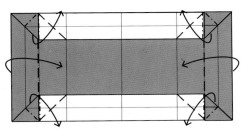

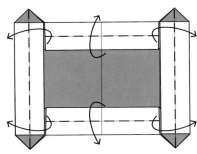

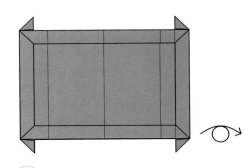

**10** Insert your chosen image. Then fold both sides in. At the same time, fold up the outer corners of the upper and lower edges.

**11** Fold the inner layers out to the folded outer edges on all sides.

**12** Turn the model over.

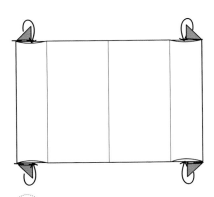

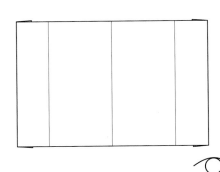

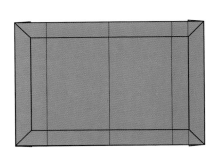

**13** Fold the corners into the model.

**14** Turn the model over.

**15** Complete.

# LOFT ROOM

The sofa and recliners form the heart of this room, a place to relax and unwind, while a pair of freestanding sculptural floor lamps add to the contemporary atmosphere. It is the perfect space for some late-night gaming, listening to music, or watching television. The room is organized around the sofa, which is designed with a deep, supportive cushion for comfortable lounging. The recliners have a more minimalist design, with a simple seat shape. The floor lamps are made with a triangular pattern that forms both the shade and feet of the lamp.

**WALLS** Little Greene, Herbes, Cocktail (left), and Spring (right)
**FLOOR** Little Greene, Bark, Heath

8³/₄
x
8³/₄in

a) 5³/₈in
b) 1¹/₈in
c) 2¹¹/₁₆in

# DEEP-CUSHIONED SOFA

**The deep-cushioned loft sofa is made by shaping the middle of the paper into a seat shape. The folding process is simplified by prefolding the front and rear sections independently. The two sections are then folded together to complete the model.**

For the pillows, follow the instructions on page 104, using a 2³/₄ x 1³/₈in rectangle for each one.

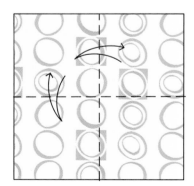

**1** Start with a square, colored side up. Fold and unfold it in half lengthwise along both axes.

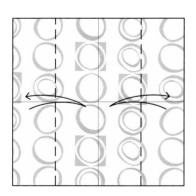

**2** Fold and unfold the left and right edges to the middle.

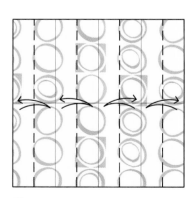

**3** Fold and unfold between the creases made previously. This will divide the paper into eight equal sections.

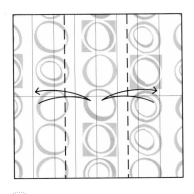

**4** Fold and unfold between the second and third creases on both sides.

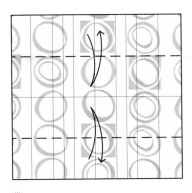

**5** Fold and unfold between the upper and lower edges and the middle.

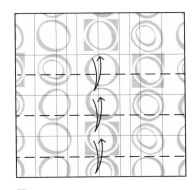

**6** Fold and unfold between the creases.

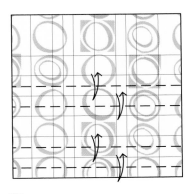

**7** Fold and unfold between the creases.

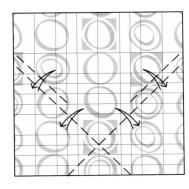

**8** Fold and unfold the diagonals as indicated.

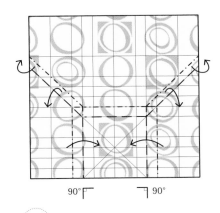

90° ⌐    ⌐ 90°

**9** Fold the sides in and out again to be perpendicular to the base. At the same time, refold the diagonal folds from step 8.

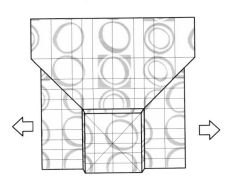

**10** Unfold the model back to a square.

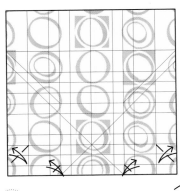

**11** Fold the diagonals where indicated. Then turn the model over.

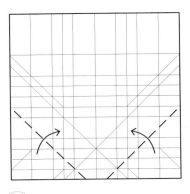

**12** Fold the lower corners in. The outer edge should align with the crease above.

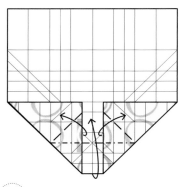

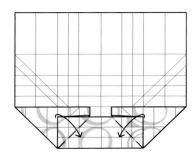

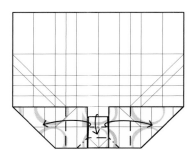

**13** Fold the lower segment up and fold the edges out.

**14** Fold the corners back down.

**15** Fold the edges out. This will cause the paper beneath to fold up and down. Then squash it flat.

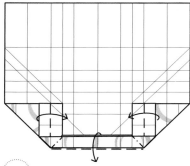

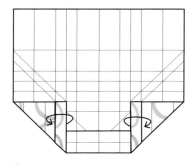

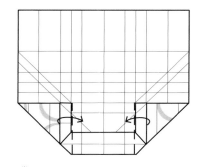

**16** Fold the lower edge down. This will cause the adjacent edges to fold in.

**17** Turn the folded edge inside out.

**18** Fold the edges back in.

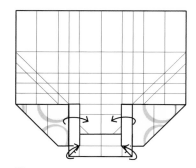

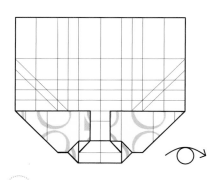

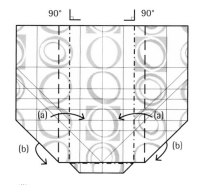

**19** Fold the edges in again. This will cause the outer corners to fold over.

**20** Turn the model over.

**21** Fold the edges in and out to be perpendicular to the middle section (a). At the same time, fold out the paper beneath (b).

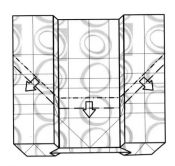

**22** Refold the diagonal folds made in step 9. Bring the rear section forward.

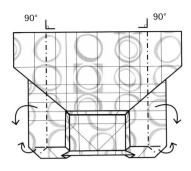

**23** Fold the edges down to be perpendicular to the upper surface.

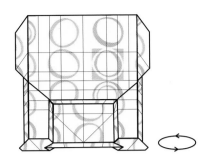

**24** Rotate the model to look at the side.

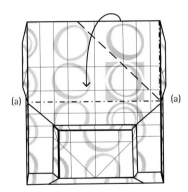

**25** Fold the corners back to be flat with the arms of the sofa.

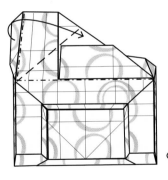

**26** Fold the edges behind, under the folded edge.

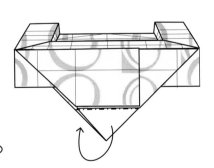

**27** Rotate the model to look at the top.

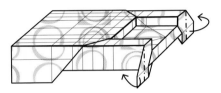

**28** Fold the back down along (a)–(a). At the same time, fold in the right edge.

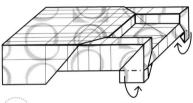

**29** Fold the left side over. Tuck the folded edge under the adjacent folded edge. Rotate the model to look at the reverse.

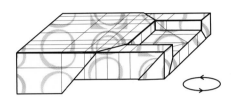

**30** Fold the corner behind.

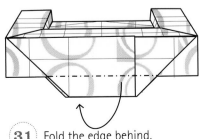

**31** Fold the edge behind.

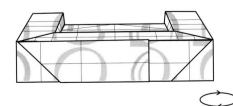

**32** Rotate the model to look at the front.

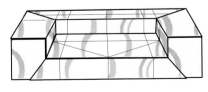

**33** Complete.

# RECLINER

**1**
SHEET

6⁵⁄₁₆
x
6⁵⁄₁₆in

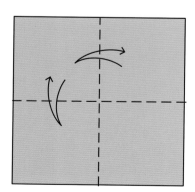

a) 1½in
b) 2⅞in
c) 3¼in

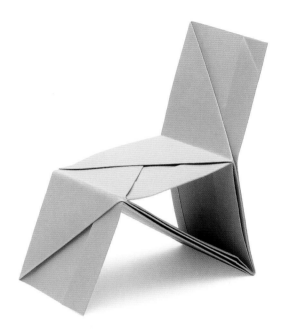

This model is an example of minimal chair design.
The overall shape is formed by tucking one edge into another;
this fold also becomes the rear legs. The leg support of the
seat also doubles as the front legs of the recliner.

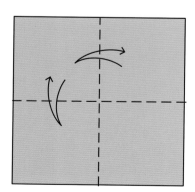

**1** Start with a square, colored side up. Fold and unfold it in half lengthwise along both axes.

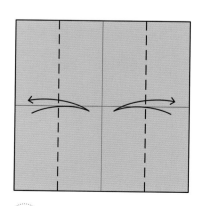

**2** Fold and unfold the left and right edges to the middle.

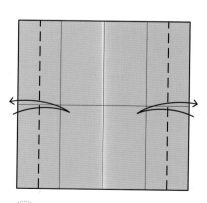

**3** Fold and unfold the edges to the adjacent creases on both sides.

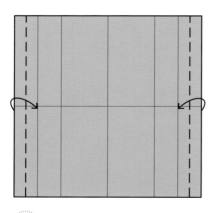

**4** Fold the outer edge in on both sides.

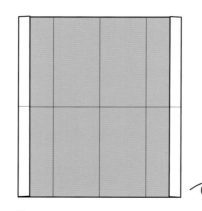

**5** Turn the model over.

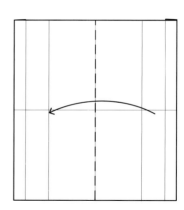

**6** Fold the right side over to touch the opposite edge.

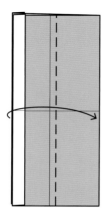

**7** Fold the upper layer over to touch the opposite edge.

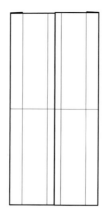

**8** Turn the model over.

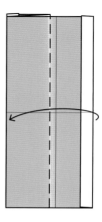

**9** Fold the upper layer over to touch the opposite edge.

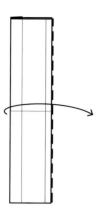

**10** Fold the front layer over.

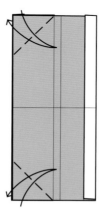

**11** Fold and unfold the corners.

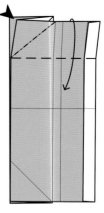

**12** Fold the upper layer down and squash the corner beneath flat.

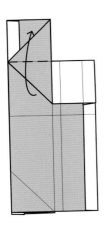

**13** Fold the edge back up again.

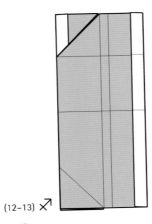

(12–13) ↗

**14** Repeat steps 12–13 on the lower edge.

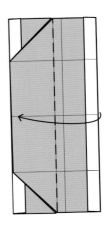

**15** Fold the upper layer back over.

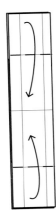

**16** Fold the upper layers in at the top and bottom.

**17** Fold and unfold along the lower edge of the upper folded section.

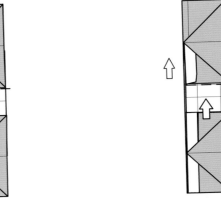

**18** Tuck the lower edge into the pocket in the section above.

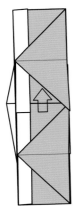

**19** Slide one section inside the other. Fold the lower section along the fold made in step 17.

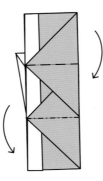

**20** Fold the upper section forward and the lower section back to shape the chair.

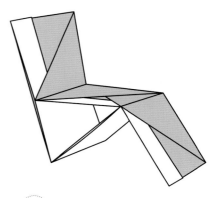

**21** Complete.

**1**
SHEET

4³/₄
x
4³/₄in

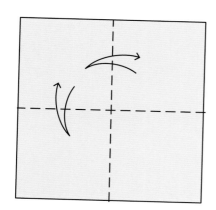

a) 1³/₁₆in
b) 3³/₈in
c) 1³/₁₆in

# FLOOR LAMP

The shade of this sculptural Japanese-style floor lamp is constructed from a series of regular folded triangles, which makes an unusual geometric shape. The triangular shape is carried through to the feet that support the lamp. The model photographed was made from white paper, so the upper side is shaded in the folding diagrams.

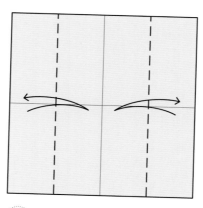

**1** Start with a square, colored side up. Fold and unfold it in half lengthwise along both axes.

**2** Fold and unfold the left and right edges to the middle.

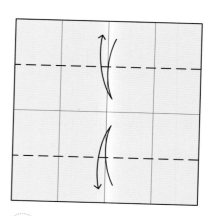

**3** Fold and unfold the upper and lower edges to the middle crease.

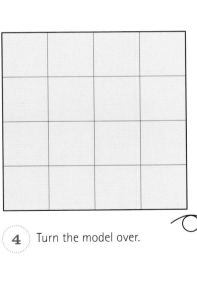

**4** Turn the model over.

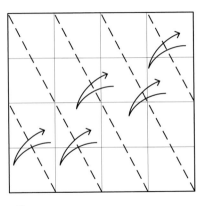

**5** Fold and unfold the diagonal folds indicated.

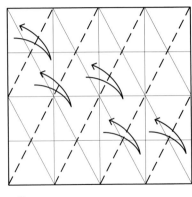

**6** Fold and unfold the diagonal folds indicated.

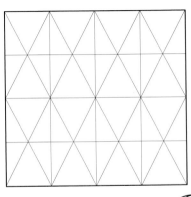

**7** Turn the model over.

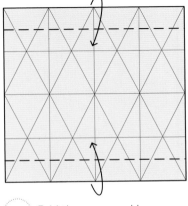

**8** Fold the upper and lower edges up to the creases made previously.

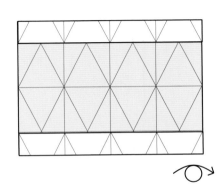

**9** Turn the model over.

**10** Fold and unfold the upper creases on both layers of the folded edge.

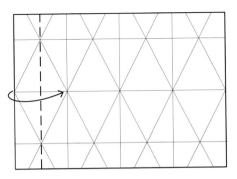

**11** Fold over the left edge to the first crease.

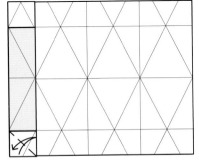

**12** Fold and unfold both layers of the lower corner.

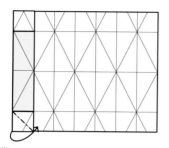

**13** Reverse-fold the corner inside the model.

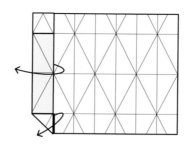

**14** Unfold the folded edge.

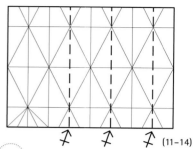

(11–14)

**15** Repeat steps 11–14 on the other sections of the lower edge.

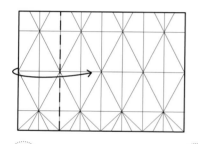

**16** Fold the left edge over at the second crease.

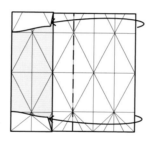

**17** Fold the right side over and tuck the outer corners beneath the folded edges of the other side.

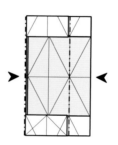

**18** Push the right side in to form a triangular prism shape.

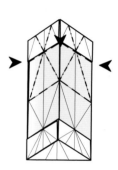

**19** Push in the edges where indicated and refold the diagonal creases.

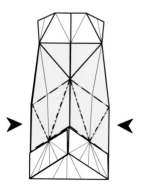

**20** Repeat the process on the lower section to shape the lamp.

**21** Reverse-fold the corners to form triangular feet.

**22** Rotate slightly to enable the model to stand up.

**23** Complete.

# TELEVISION

The flat-screen television in the loft room is made in the same way as the one in the living room. The only difference is that here it is mounted on the wall with double-sided tape, rather than being free-standing.

For the television, follow the instructions on page 29, using a 6⁷⁄₈ x 6⁷⁄₈in square.

# RUG

Offcuts of paper can be utilized to make throw pillows, or—even easier—rugs for the floor. Choose a pattern or color that works with your furniture and set design, and simply cut it to the required size.

For the rug, cut a piece of paper to approximately 5¹⁄₂ x 3in.

# FAMILY DINING ROOM

The family dining room is an informal, functional eating space, where all of the household can gather together at meal times. At the heart of the space is a large rectangular table that comfortably seats six to eight and doubles as a surface to do homework and craft projects. With chairs at both ends and benches on either side, the layout allows more people to fit around the table for a shared eating experience. A traditional hutch is the place to store china, flatware, and table linen. The room has a fun, light-hearted feel, with the multicolored donut-patterned table setting the tone, and the benches and chairs made in complementary colors.

**WALLS** Farrow & Ball, Toile Trellis, BP620 (left), and BP669 (right)
**FLOOR** Farrow & Ball, Polka Square, BP1053

8 ¹¹/₁₆
x
6⁷/₈in

a
b | c

Dining Table
a) 5¼in
b) 2¼in
c) 4in

Desk
a) 4⁵/₈in
b) 2¼in
c) 4in

# RECTANGULAR DINING TABLE

The folding process used to make the octagonal dining table on page 38 turns the corners of the starting square into the table's legs. A longer table can be made by applying the folding process to the corners of a rectangle. Any increase in the length of the starting rectangle will cause a corresponding increase in the length of the rectangular dining table.

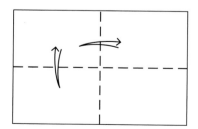

**1** Start with a rectangle, colored side down. Fold and unfold it in half lengthwise along both axes.

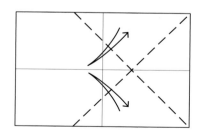

**2** Fold and unfold the lower right corner to the upper edge and the upper right corner to the lower edge, making two diagonal folds.

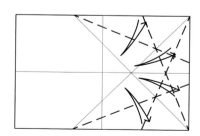

**3** Fold and unfold between the edges of the paper and the diagonal creases made previously.

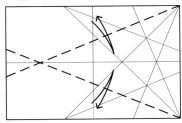

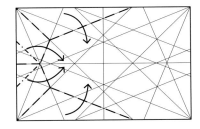

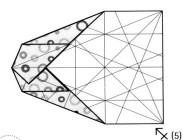

**4** Fold and unfold between the upper and lower edges and the diagonal creases. Repeat steps 1–4 on the left side.

**5** Fold the left outer edges in, repeating steps 5–9 of the octagonal dining table on page 39.

**6** Fold in the right side in the same way.

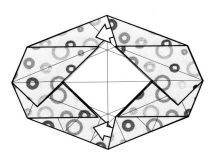

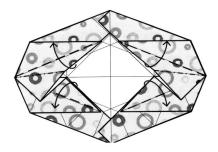

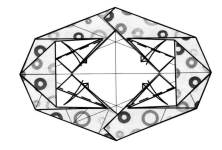

**7** Reverse-fold out the trapped paper and flatten.

**8** Fold the edges out and open out the folded triangle. (This is step 15 of the octagonal dining table on page 40.)

**9** Fold and unfold the four points where indicated.

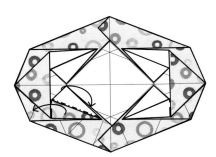

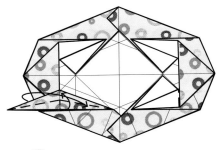

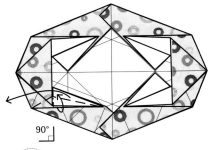

**10** Fold one point over along the adjacent folded edge. This will cause the paper above to fold over.

**11** Fold the point back. At the same time, fold the edge in to narrow the point.

**12** Fold the points back to the left and fold the outer edge in. This will cause the point to stand perpendicular to the base.

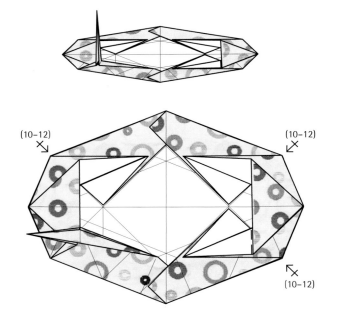

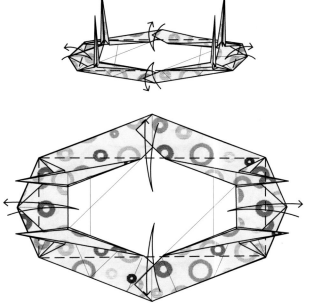

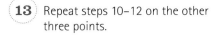

**13** Repeat steps 10–12 on the other three points.

**14** Fold and unfold the corners of the table.

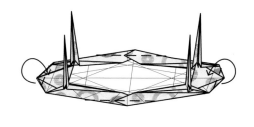

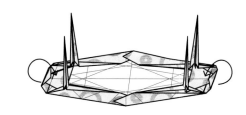

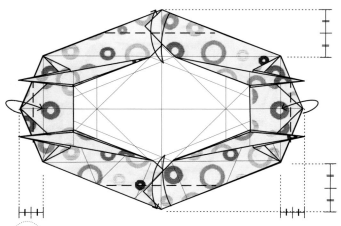

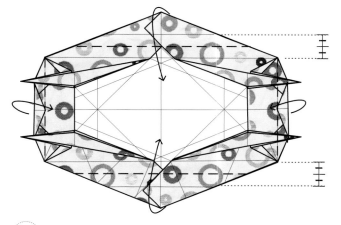

**15** Fold the left and right corners in to the creases made previously. Then fold and unfold the upper and lower corners in to the creases.

**16** Fold the edges in where indicated. The left and right edges should be perpendicular to the base.

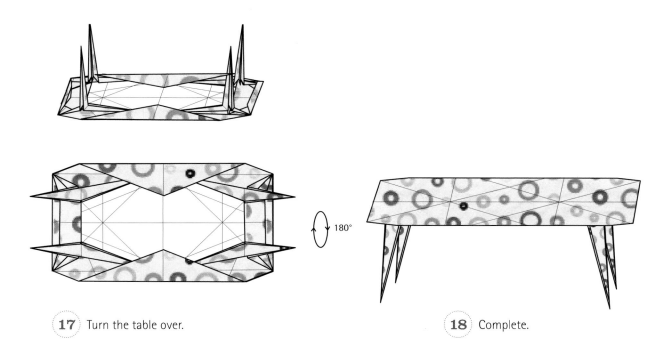

**17** Turn the table over.

**18** Complete.

## CONTINUE FOR MAKING THE DESK ON PAGE 84

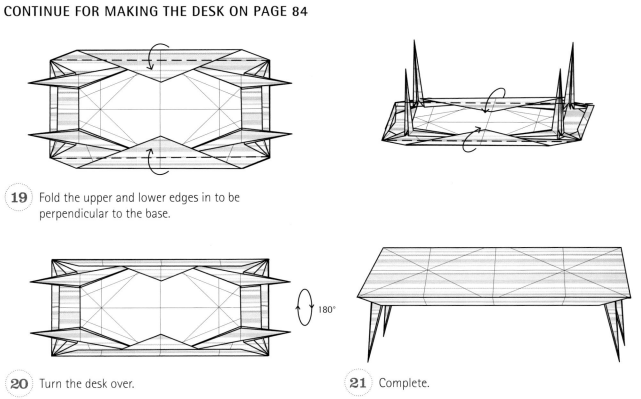

**19** Fold the upper and lower edges in to be perpendicular to the base.

**20** Turn the desk over.

**21** Complete.

Bench
6⁵⁄₁₆ x 6⁵⁄₁₆in

TV Stand
6⁷⁄₈ x 6⁷⁄₈in

Bench
a) 4³⁄₄in
b) 1¹⁄₄in
c) 1⁵⁄₈in

TV Bench
a) 5¹⁄₈in
b) 1³⁄₈in
c) 1³⁄₄in

# BENCH

On a similar premise to the dining tables, the corners of the starting square become the legs of the bench. However, the folding process creates a longer seat by making shorter legs. The height of the bench can be adjusted by folding in the tips of the legs. The bench also doubles as a TV stand (see page 31).

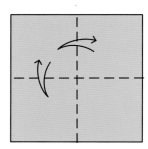

**1** Start with a square, colored side up. Fold and unfold it in half lengthwise along both axes.

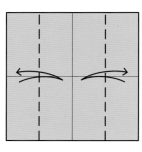

**2** Fold and unfold the left and right edges to the middle. Then turn the model over.

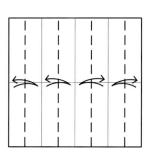

**3** Fold and unfold between the creases. This will divide the paper into eight equal sections.

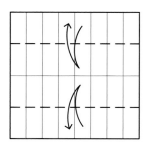

**4** Fold and unfold the upper and lower edges to the middle crease.

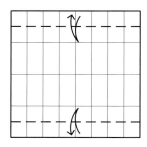

**5** Fold and unfold between the creases.

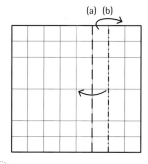

**6** Fold the right side over at (a) and back over at (b).

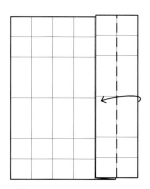

**7** Fold the edge over.

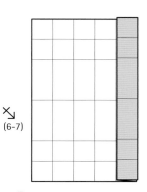

**8** Repeat steps 6–7 on the left side.

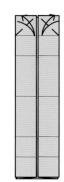

**9** Fold and unfold the upper corners on the front and rear layers.

**10** Reverse-fold the corners into the model on the front and rear layers.

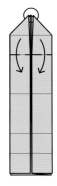

**11** Fold the upper layer down. Open out and flatten the layer beneath.

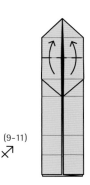

**12** Fold the corners back up again. Then repeat steps 9–11 on the lower section.

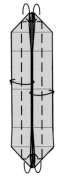

**13** Fold the upper layers of the inner section to the outer edges. This will cause the corners to fold over.

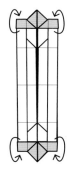

**14** Turn the folded tips inside out.

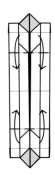

**15** Fold the points back into the middle.

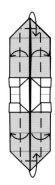

**16** Fold the edges out. This will open out the upper and lower corners.

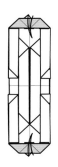

**17** Fold and unfold the upper and lower edges.

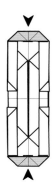

**18** Reverse the edges into the model to flatten the ends.

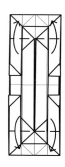 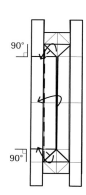 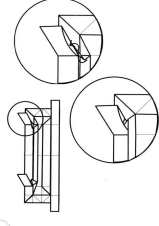

**19** Fold the legs back out again.

**20** Fold the legs up to be perpendicular to the seat. At the same time, fold the inner edge up.

**21** The previous fold will cause small triangular folds where the edge touches the legs. Tuck these into the layers of paper in the legs.

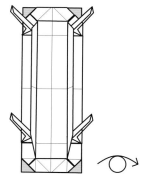 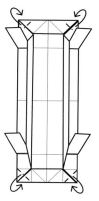 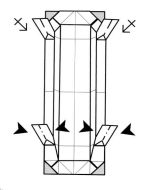

(20–21)

**22** Repeat step 20–21 on the other side.

**23** Fold the upper layer of the outer corners behind to tighten the ends.

**24** Pinch the legs together.

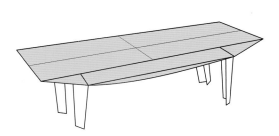

**25** Turn the model over and stand the bench up.

**26** Complete.

# DINING CHAIR

6⁵/₁₆
x
6⁵/₁₆in

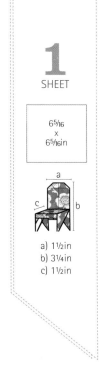

a) 1½in
b) 3¼in
c) 1½in

The legs of this dining chair are folded from the edge
of the paper, rather than the corners. The model has some
interesting features, including using the familiar triangular
folded shape to form the legs, and using some three-
dimensional folding methods to give it rigidity.

**1** Start with a square, colored
side up. Fold it into three
equal sections along both axes
and then unfold so the square
is divided into nine equal
sections. (See throw pillow
steps 1–7 on pages 24–5.)

**2** Fold the model diagonally
as indicated, ensuring the
ends of the folds align with
the creases made previously.
Then turn the model over
left to right.

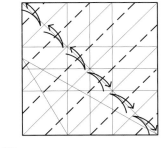

**3** Fold and unfold between
the diagonal creases
made previously.

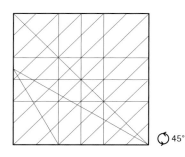

(2-3)

↙ ✕

↻ 45°

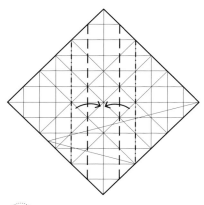

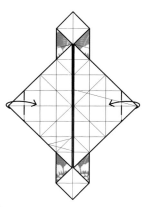

④ Repeat steps 2–3 on the opposite axis. Then rotate the model 45° anticlockwise.

⑤ Fold the two sides in and then out again.

⑥ Fold the outer corners in on both sides.

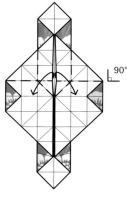

90°

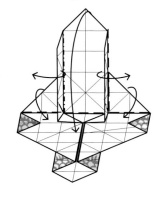

⑦ Fold the top section up to be perpendicular to the lower section. At the same time, fold out the inner edges.

⑧ Fold the edges out again and flatten the perpendicular section.

⑨ Fold the lower section up. At the same time, fold the edges out where indicated and flatten.

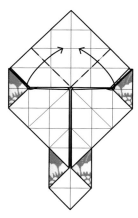

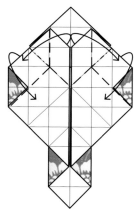

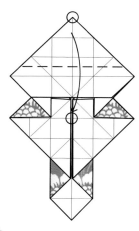

⑩ Fold the corners of the middle section in.

⑪ Fold the edges back and fold the adjacent edges in.

⑫ Fold the point down to touch the point where indicated.

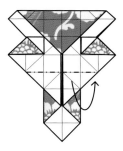

**13** Fold the lower section behind.

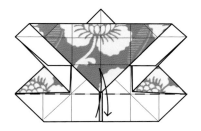

**14** Fold and then unfold the lower edge into the model.

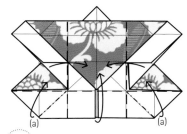

**15** Fold the left, right, and lower edges in. At the same time, fold in the corners (a).

**16** Fold the section back.

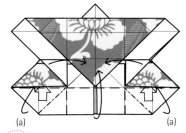

**17** Fold the edges in again, repeating step 15. At the same time, fold the corners in and under the adjacent pockets (a).

**18** Turn the model over, top to bottom.

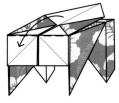

**19** Fold the top section back up.

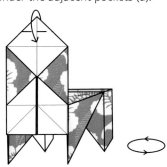

**20** Fold the tip down. Then rotate the model to face the front.

**21** Fold the front edge over.

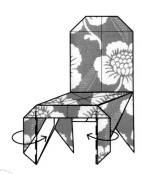

**22** Fold the sides back over again.

**23** Fold the edges back and tuck them into the adjacent pockets in the legs.

**24** Complete.

DINING CHAIR    75

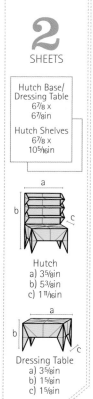

Hutch Base/
Dressing Table
6⅞ x
6⅞in

Hutch Shelves
6⅞ x
10⁵⁄₁₆in

Hutch
a) 3⅝in
b) 5⅜in
c) 1¹¹⁄₁₆in

Dressing Table
a) 3⅝in
b) 1⅝in
c) 1⅝in

# HUTCH

The hutch is a two-piece model. The lower section, which also forms the dressing table on page 107, is made from a square and the upper section is made from a 3 x 2 rectangle. The folding technique for the lower section can also be used to make a square table by leaving out steps 15–16. The rectangle used for the upper section should be as wide as the square used for the lower section. More shelves can be added by increasing the length of this rectangle.

## HUTCH BASE

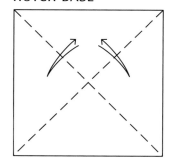

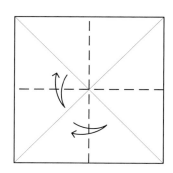

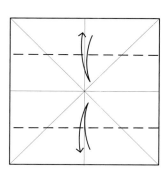

1  Start with a square, colored side down. Fold and unfold it in half diagonally along both axes.

2  Fold and unfold the square in half lengthwise along both axes.

3  Fold and unfold the upper and lower edges to the middle crease.

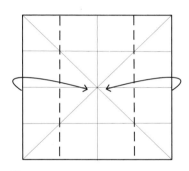

**4** Fold the left and right edges to the middle crease.

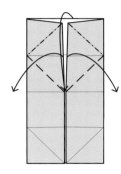

**5** Fold the top section down and open out the upper layers.

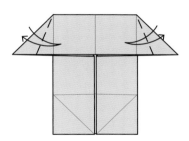

**6** Fold and unfold the outer edges to the middle crease.

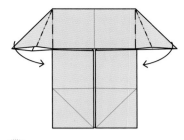

**7** Fold the corners up, separate the layers, and squash the points flat.

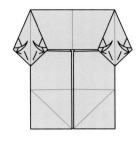

**8** Fold and unfold the edges of the points to the middle.

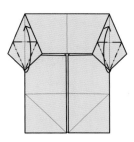

**9** Fold the upper layers of the points up and reverse the creases made previously.

(5–9)

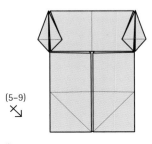

**10** Repeat steps 5–9 on the lower section.

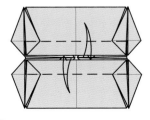

**11** Fold and unfold the inner edges.

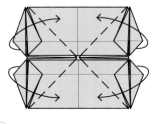

**12** Fold the outer edges in diagonally.

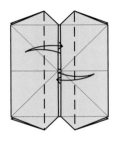

**13** Fold and unfold the inner edges.

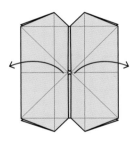

**14** Unfold back to a square.

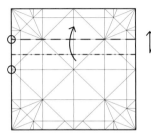

**15** Fold the lower section up and down again.

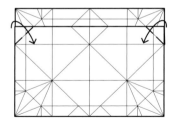

**16** Fold the outer corners of the middle fold in.

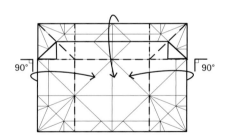

**17** Fold the edges in on three sides to stand perpendicular to the base.

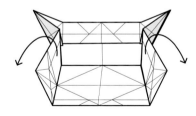

**18** Fold the model flat again.

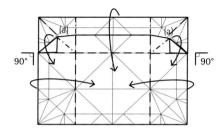

**19** Fold the edges back in. At the same time, fold the outer edges of the folded edge (a) into the model.

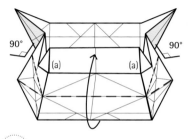

**20** Fold the front edge up to be perpendicular to the base.

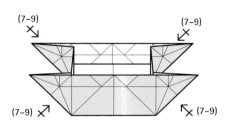

**21** Refold the corners as folded previously in steps 7–9.

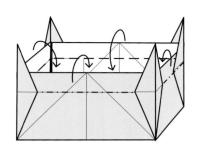

**22** Fold the edges back in.

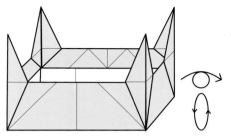

**23** Turn the model over.

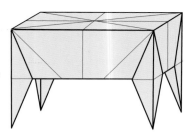

**24** Complete.

## SHELVES

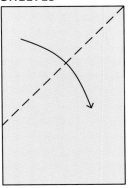

1. Start with a 2 x 3 rectangle, colored side up. Fold the upper left corner down to make the upper edge touch the right side.

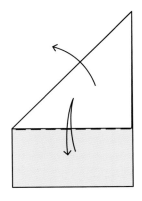

2. Fold and unfold the lower section along the folded edge. Then unfold back to a rectangle.

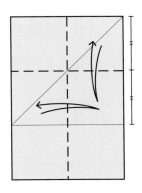

3. Fold and unfold the middle crease lengthwise. Then fold and unfold between the upper edge and the crease made in step 2.

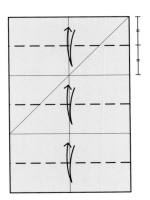

4. Fold and unfold between the creases made previously.

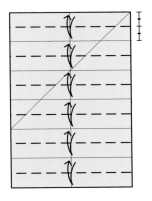

5. Fold and unfold between the creases made previously.

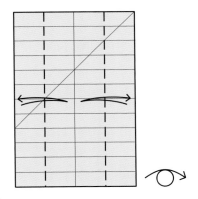

6. Fold and unfold the left and right edges to the middle crease. Then turn the model over.

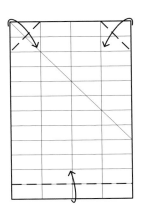

7. Fold the upper corners in and the lower edge up.

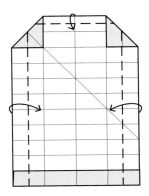

8. Fold the sides and top edge in.

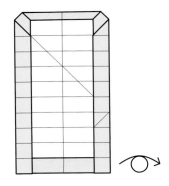

9. Turn the model over.

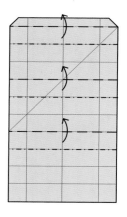

**10** Fold the model up and down where indicated.

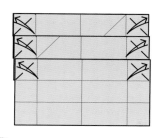

**11** Fold and unfold the six outer corners.

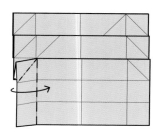

**12** Fold the left edge over, and open out and flatten the corner folded previously.

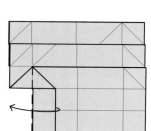

**13** Fold the edge back again. This will reverse the folded corner.

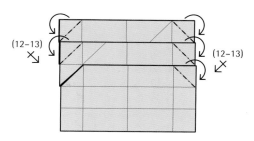

**14** Repeat steps 12–13 on the other five corners.

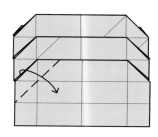

**15** Fold over the lower left corner and open up the paper beneath to stand perpendicular to the base.

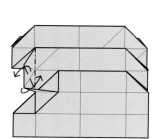

**16** Flatten the raised section.

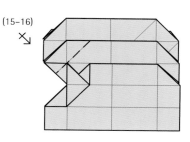

**17** Repeat steps 15–16 on the next corner.

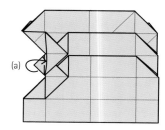

**18** Fold the corner (a) underneath the adjacent folded triangle.

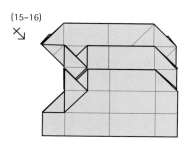

**19** Repeat steps 15–16 on the next corner.

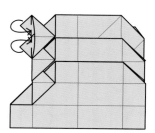

**20** Fold the corners underneath the adjacent triangle.

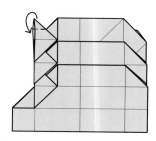

**21** Fold the tip of the upper corner in. (This is optional— see note, opposite.)

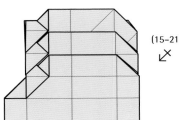

**22** Repeat steps 15–21 on the right side.

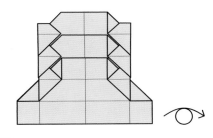

**23** Turn the model over.

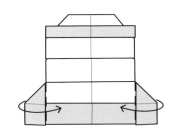

**24** Fold the edges in.

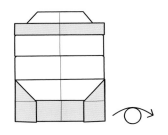

**25** Turn the model over.

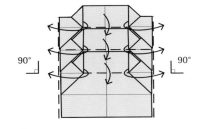

**26** Fold down the shelves and open out the sides to be perpendicular to the base.

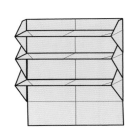

**27** Complete.

## PUTTING THE BASE AND SHELVES TOGETHER

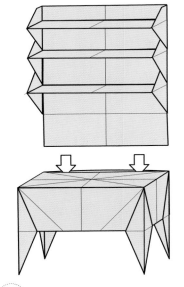

**1** Insert the lower edge of the shelf section into the pocket at the back of the base.

**2** Complete.

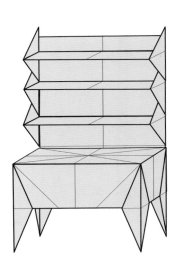

The model shown in the photographs on pages 65 and 76 has a pointed top edge. This was made by leaving out step 21.

# WORKSPACE

The home workspace is organized around the computer, which sits on a desk with an Anglepoise-style reading lamp. The gray-and-yellow walls create a neutral, fresh feel to focus the mind, while the orange lamp and turquoise chair add some fun to the room and inspire the creative side of an enthusiastic author. The armchair is a neat, compact design and could be made in a variety of patterns and colors (see pages 6–7). The bookcase has been mounted on the wall but could just as easily stand on the floor, and the reading lamp could be made larger as a freestanding lamp to light the room.

**WALLS** Mini Moderns, Vanessa Wallpaper, Mustard
**FLOOR** Malabar, China Grass Wallpaper, Sisal Rice Wpsis01

# DESK

The desk is made with a slight variation to the rectangular dining table (see page 66), itself a version of the octagonal dining table (see page 38). The subtle striped pattern has been chosen to tone with the walls.

For the desk, follow the instructions on page 66, using a 6⁷⁄₈ x 8¹¹⁄₁₆in rectangle.

# DESK CHAIR

This dot-patterned turquoise chair adds a splash of contrasting color, bringing an energetic vibe to the room. It's an example of the classic dining chair on page 42, a versatile design with simple lines that works well in most room sets.

For the chair, follow the instructions on page 42, using a 6⁵⁄₁₆ x 6⁵⁄₁₆in square.

# COMPUTER SCREEN AND KEYBOARD

Keyboard
4³/₄ x
3¹/₈in

Computer
Screen
6⁵/₁₆ x
6⁵/₁₆in

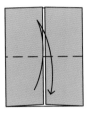

a

b

c

a) 2³/₈in
b) ³/₁₆in
c) 1³/₁₆in

The screen of this two-part model is the television on page 29, and the keyboard is a folded wedge (see below). This shows how a minimal number of folds can be used to capture the character of an object.

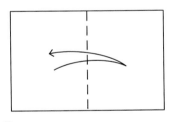

**1** For the keyboard, start with a 3 x 2 rectangle, colored side down. Fold and unfold it in half lengthwise.

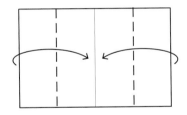

**2** Fold the left and right sides into the middle.

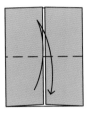

**3** Fold and unfold along the middle widthwise.

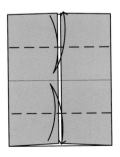

**4** Fold and unfold the upper and lower edges to the middle crease.

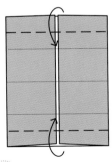

**5** Fold the edges in to stand perpendicular to the base.

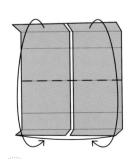

**6** Fold the model in half widthwise and tuck one edge into the other.

For the computer screen, follow the instructions on page 29, using a 6⁵/₁₆ x 6⁵/₁₆in square.

**7** Keyboard complete.

3⁷⁄₁₆
x
3⁷⁄₁₆in

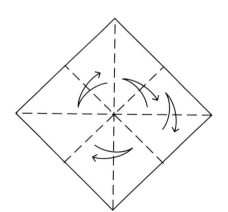

a) 1³⁄₈in
b) 2in
c) ⁷⁄₈in

# READING LAMP

This model works on the diagonal axis of a square,
the lamp shade and base being made from opposite corners.
To make sure the model stands up, make the base as flat as
possible and adjust the angle of the lamp. If you wish to make
a freestanding floor lamp, 4in tall, use a 6⁷⁄₈ x 6⁷⁄₈in square.

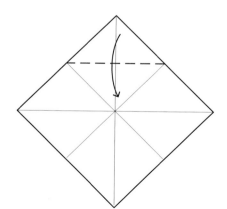

1 Start with a square, colored side down. Fold and unfold it in half lengthwise and diagonally along both axes.

2 Fold the upper corner to the middle of the square.

3 Fold and unfold the upper left and right edges to the middle creases made previously.

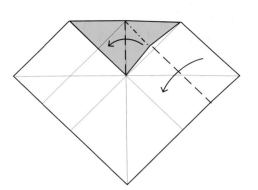

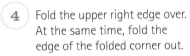

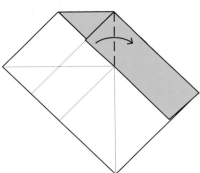

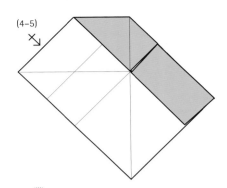

**4** Fold the upper right edge over. At the same time, fold the edge of the folded corner out.

**5** Fold the triangle back over.

**6** Repeat steps 4–5 on the other side.

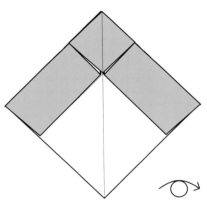

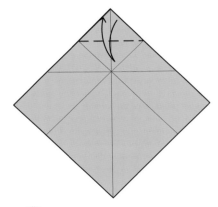

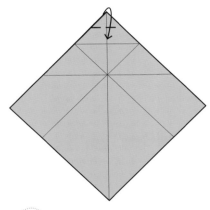

**7** Turn the model over.

**8** Fold and unfold the upper triangle down to the point where the creases intersect.

**9** Fold the upper corner down to the crease made previously.

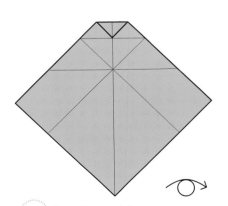

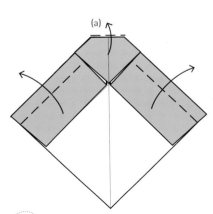

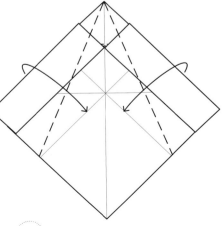

**10** Turn the model over.

**11** Fold the upper layer up along the folded edge (a). This will cause the folded edges below to fold out where indicated.

**12** Fold the outer edges in to the middle crease.

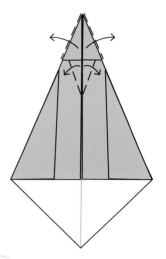 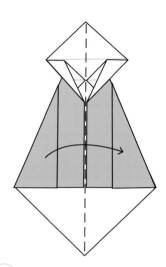 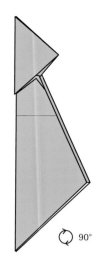

**13** Fold out the edges of the upper section. This will cause the paper in the layer beneath to fold out.

**14** Fold the model in half lengthwise.

**15** Rotate the model 90° clockwise.

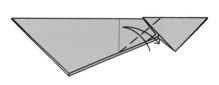 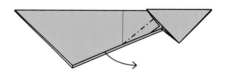 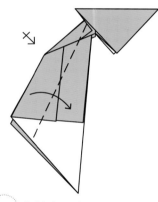

**16** Fold and unfold between the crease and the folded edge beneath.

**17** Reverse-fold the left side into the model along the crease made previously.

**18** Fold the edge over in front and behind.

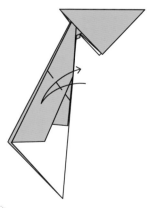 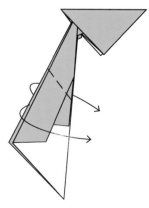 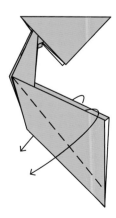

**19** Fold and unfold diagonally about halfway down the longer section.

**20** Fold the lower edges of the longer section inside out along the crease made previously.

**21** Fold the edges over in front and behind.

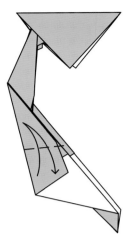

**22** Fold and unfold.

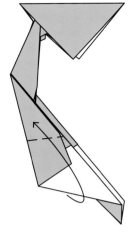

**23** Fold up the outer layer of the lower section, open the point and flatten.

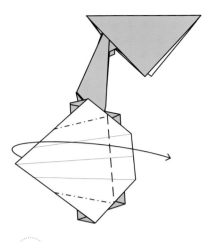

**24** Fold the open section back and fold the edges in.

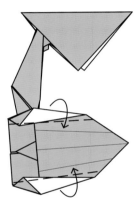

**25** Fold the outer edges of the base in.

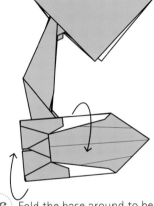

**26** Fold the base around to be perpendicular to the upper section of the model.

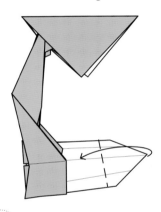

**27** Fold the outer corner in and tuck it underneath the adjacent folded edge.

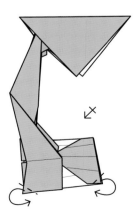

**28** Fold the corners of the base beneath at the front and back.

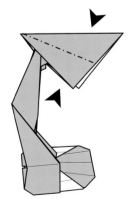

**29** Pinch the upper section and shape the lampshade.

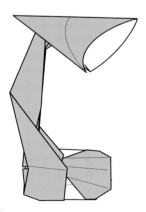

**30** Complete.

8 ¹¹/₁₆
x
6 ⁷/₈in

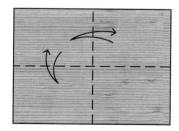

a) 3 ¹/₈in
b) 2in
c) ³/₄in

# BOOKCASE

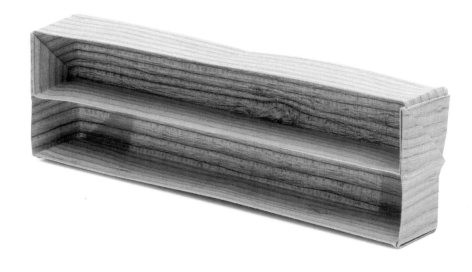

The bookcase is a flexible model that can be extended upward or made narrower by changing the dimensions of the starting rectangle (see page 92). Attach it to the wall of your set with double-sided tape for a wall-mounted bookcase, as here, or use it as a low-level freestanding unit. Here it is made in a paper that mimics the appearance of natural wood, but instead you could use a plain bold color for a more contemporary look.

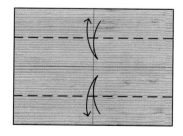

**1** Start with a rectangle, colored side up. Fold and unfold it in half lengthwise along both axes.

**2** Fold and unfold the upper and lower edges to the middle crease.

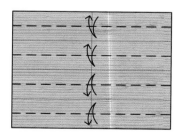

**3** Fold and unfold between the creases made previously. This will divide the paper into eight equal sections.

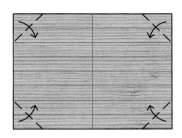

**4** Fold the corners in. The edges should align with the creases folded in the previous step.

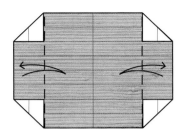

**5** Fold and unfold both sides in along the edges of the folded corners.

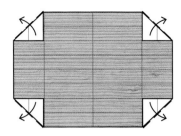

**6** Unfold the corners.

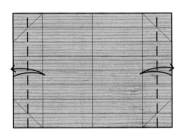

**7** Fold and unfold between the outer edges and the creases folded in step 5.

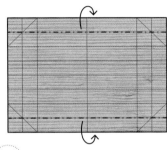

**8** Fold the upper and lower edges behind along the creases indicated.

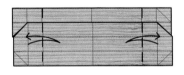

**9** Fold the upper edge down along (a–a) and then up again along (b–b).

**10** Fold the corners in.

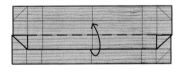

**11** Fold the edge up.

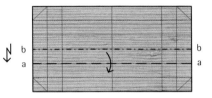

**12** Fold and unfold the sides in and back again.

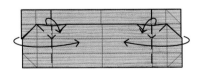

**13** Fold the sides in. At the same time, make two diagonal folds.

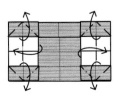

**14** Open out the paper in the folded edges.

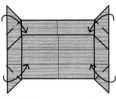

**15** Fold the corners in.

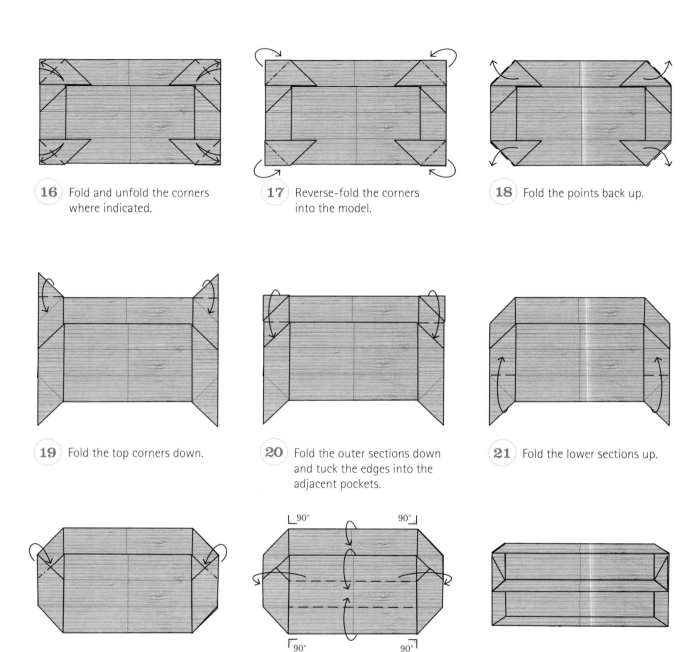

**16** Fold and unfold the corners where indicated.

**17** Reverse-fold the corners into the model.

**18** Fold the points back up.

**19** Fold the top corners down.

**20** Fold the outer sections down and tuck the edges into the adjacent pockets.

**21** Fold the lower sections up.

**22** Tuck the corners behind into the pocket beneath.

**23** Open the model by folding the upper and lower edges in and the sides out. The shelves should stand perpendicular to the base.

**24** Complete.

**EXTENDING THE BOOKCASE** The two-shelf bookcase shown is made from a landscape rectangle divided into eight equal sections, with each shelf using three of the eight sections. Shelves can be added to the model by increasing the shorter dimension of the starting rectangle, adding three-eighths of a rectangle for each additional shelf. To make the bookcase narrower, decrease the longer dimension of the starting rectangle.

# ARMCHAIR

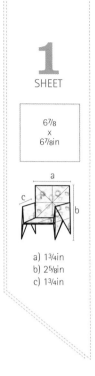

**1**
SHEET

6⁷⁄₈
x
6⁷⁄₈in

a) 1³⁄₄in
b) 2⁵⁄₈in
c) 1³⁄₄in

This armchair has been included in the workspace as a comfortable chair for reading or somewhere for a visitor to sit. However, it is a generic armchair that could be included in any room set as part of the furniture collection if it is done in a color or pattern that ties in with the décor and other models (see pages 6–7).

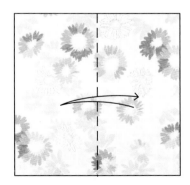

1  Start with a square, colored side up. Fold and unfold it in half lengthwise.

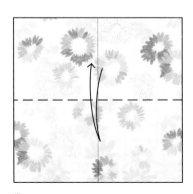

2  Fold and unfold the square in half along the opposite axis.

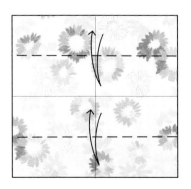

3  Fold and unfold the upper and lower edges to the middle crease.

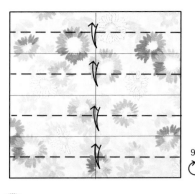

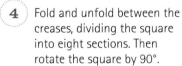

**4** Fold and unfold between the creases, dividing the square into eight sections. Then rotate the square by 90°.

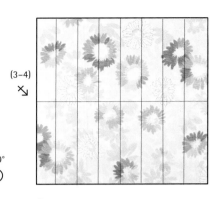

**5** Repeat steps 3–4 to divide the other axis into eight.

(3–4)

90°

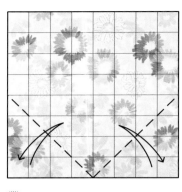

**6** Fold and unfold the lower corners to the middle. Then turn the model over.

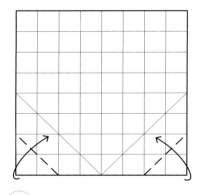

**7** Fold the lower corners in where indicated.

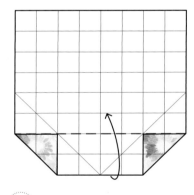

**8** Fold two-eighths of the lower section up.

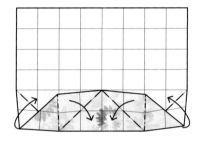

**9** Fold the upper edge of the folded section down diagonally. This will cause the outer corners to fold up.

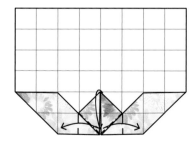

**10** Fold the inner corners out. This will cause the upper point to open out and fold down.

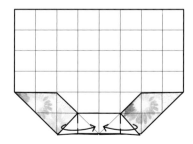

**11** Fold the corners back again.

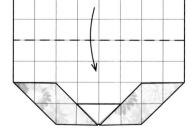

**12** Fold the upper two-eighths of the model down.

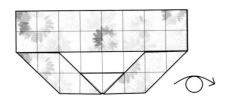

**13** Turn the model over.

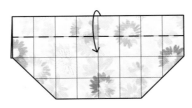

**14** Fold the upper segment over.

**15** Fold and unfold where indicated.

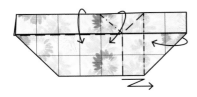

**16** Fold the right side over and back again. At the same time, fold the upper left edge down.

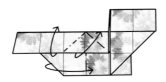

**17** Fold the left side to the right. At the same time, open up the folded edge and fold it over. This mirrors step 16.

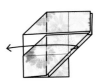

**18** Fold the upper layer back over to the left.

**19** Turn the model over.

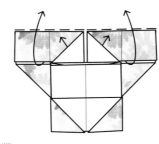

**20** Fold up the paper in the upper section. This will cause the trapped paper to fold out.

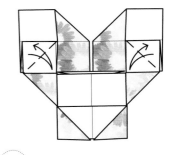

**21** Fold and unfold the outer corners of the upper middle section.

**22** Fold the lower corners out.

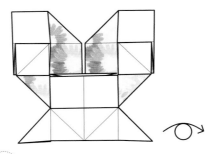

**23** Turn the model over.

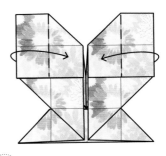

**24** Fold the upper edges in. This will cause the lower layer to fold over along the crease made in step 21.

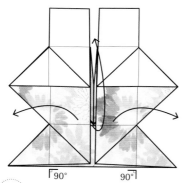  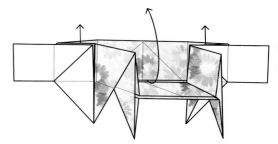

**25** Fold the edges out to be perpendicular to the middle of the model.

**26** Fold out the points from behind to be parallel with the middle section.

**27** Reverse-fold out the trapped layer from the middle of the model.

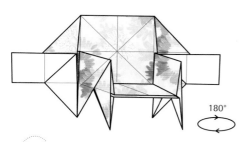 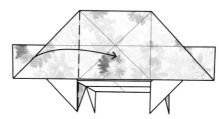 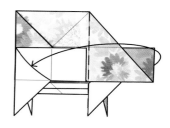

**28** Rotate the model 180° to work on the back.

**29** Fold the left edge in.

**30** Fold the right edge over. Tuck the outer edge into the pocket on the other side.

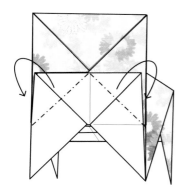 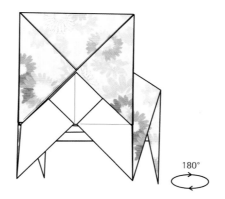 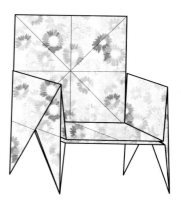

**31** Fold the corners behind.

**32** Rotate the model 180°.

**33** Complete.

# BEDROOM

A color scheme of soft gray-toned blues, lilacs, and greens promotes relaxation and enhances the feeling of comfort in this romantic bedroom. The bed is the focal point of the room, with the rest of the furniture organized around it and reflecting its design. Feel free to bring in different chairs or items from other sets to develop the room. Alternatively, the same pieces of furniture made up in other color schemes and patterns will create very different atmospheres. Try experimenting with reds and yellows for a more vibrant feel, for example.

**WALLS** Farrow & Ball, Ocelot, BP3705 (left), and Wisteria, BP2217 (right)
**FLOOR** Farrow & Ball, Lattice, BP3502

# BED

Bed
1 x
8¹¹/₁₆ x
8¹¹/₁₆ in

Bedcover
1 x
6½ x
6½ in

Pillows
2 x
2³/₁₆ x
4⁵/₁₆ in

a) 4⁵/₁₆ in
b) 4⁵/₁₆ in
c) 2⁵/₈ in

The bed is a four-piece model. The bed base is made from one square of paper, with the bedcover and pillows being made from smaller sheets proportional to the size of the starting square for the base (see below). Have fun trying out different colors and patterns for all the component parts.

## BED ELEMENTS

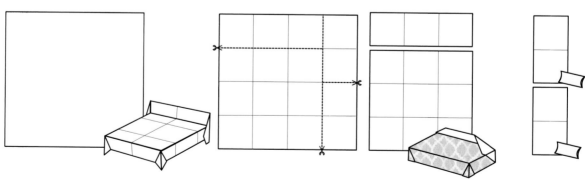

The bed base is made from a square.

To make matching bedcover and pillows, use a square the same size as for the bed base. Fold it into four equal sections along each axis.

The bedcover is made from a 3 x 3 square.

The pillows can then be made from the two remaining 1 x 2 rectangles.

## BED BASE

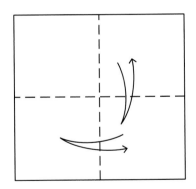

1. Start with a square, colored side down. Fold and unfold it in half lengthwise along both axes.

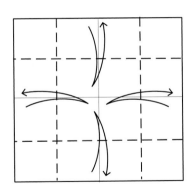

2. Fold and unfold the four outer edges in to touch the middle crease.

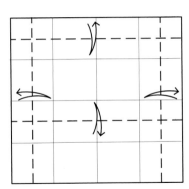

3. Fold and unfold between the creases made previously.

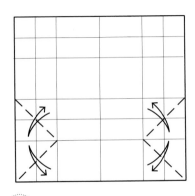

4. Fold and unfold diagonally where indicated.

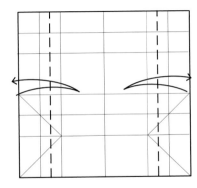

5. Fold and unfold the sides lengthwise between the creases made previously.

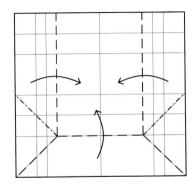

6. Fold the edges in on three sides. The lower section should end up on top.

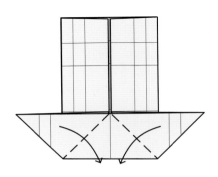

7. Fold the corners over to point downward.

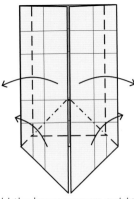

8. Fold the lower corners out to either side. At the same time, fold out the upper layers to the left and right along the creases made previously.

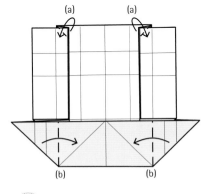

9. Fold the corners over at (a), and then fold the corners in at (b).

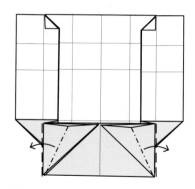

**10** Fold the corners up to be perpendicular to the base, separate the layers, and flatten.

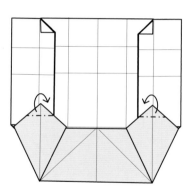

**11** Fold the tips of the flattened corners behind.

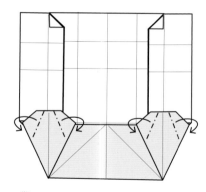

**12** Fold the edges behind on both sides.

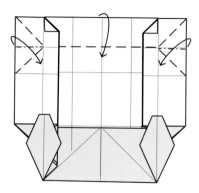

**13** Fold the upper edge over. At the same time, fold in the corners.

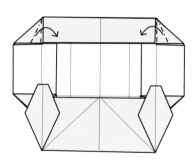

**14** Fold the corners up, separate the layers, and flatten.

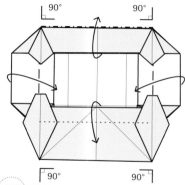

**15** Fold the edges in to be perpendicular to the base of the model.

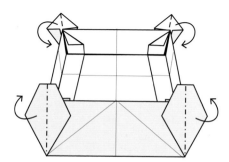

**16** Fold the edges of the legs around to be flush with the base of the bed.

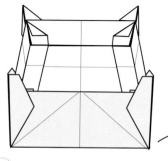

**17** Turn the model over.

**18** Bed base complete.

## BEDCOVER

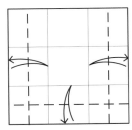

1. Start with a square, colored side down. Fold it into thirds along both axes (see steps 1–7 on pages 24–5). Fold and unfold the edges to the third creases.

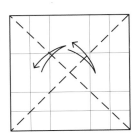

2. Fold and unfold diagonally along both axes.

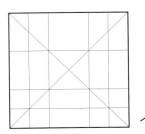

3. Turn the model over.

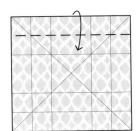

4. Fold the upper edge over.

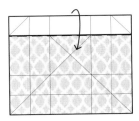

5. Fold it over again.

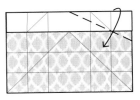

6. Fold the upper right corner over.

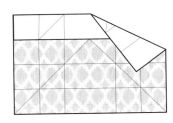

7. Turn the model over.

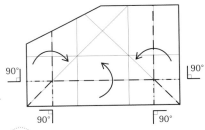

8. Fold the sides and lower edge in to be perpendicular to the central section. Pinch the corners together.

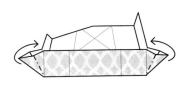

9. Fold the corners in and squash flat.

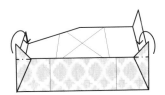

10. Fold the corners over to lock the model together.

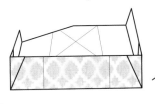

11. Turn the model over.

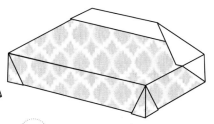

12. Bedcover complete.

# PILLOWS

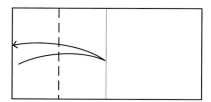

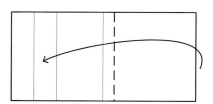

**1** Start with a 2 x 1 rectangle, colored side down. Fold and unfold the left edge to the middle.

**2** Fold and unfold between the left edge and the crease made previously.

**3** Fold the right edge over to the crease made in step 2.

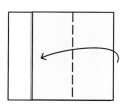

**4** Fold the right edge over.

**5** Fold the left edge over.

**6** Fold in the ends. This will open out the tube and make it three-dimensional.

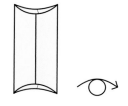

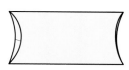

**7** Turn over and rotate.

**8** Pillow complete.

**9** Slot the bedcover over the lower part of the bed base and place the pillows at the top of the bed.

# BEDSIDE TABLE

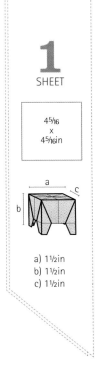

**1**
SHEET

4⁵/₁₆
x
4⁵/₁₆in

a) 1½in
b) 1½in
c) 1½in

The construction technique for this model is similar to the dressing table overleaf and the hutch on page 76, with the four legs of the table being made from the corners of a square. However, by condensing the design and dividing the square into three, this model is given a different appearance.

Fold in progress.

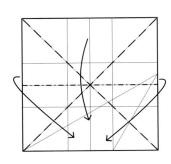

1. Start with a square, colored side down. Complete steps 1–7 of the throw pillow on pages 24–5. Then fold in the left and right edges along the diagonal creases.

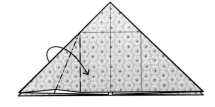

2. Fold the left corner up, separate the layers, and flatten.

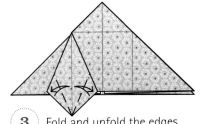

3. Fold and unfold the edges of the flattened point to the middle.

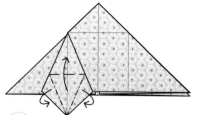

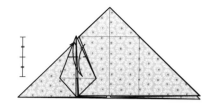

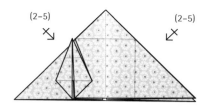

**4** Fold the point up. At the same time, fold the edges of the point behind.

**5** Fold and unfold the point between the tip and the fold made in step 4.

**6** Repeat steps 2–5 on the other three corners.

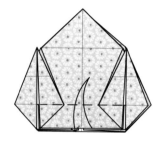

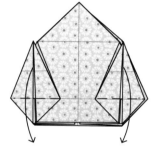

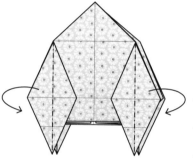

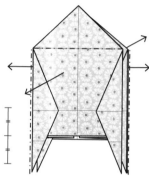

**7** Fold and unfold the lower edge on all four sides.

**8** Fold the four points down.

**9** Fold the outer edges of the folded points behind on all four points.

**10** Open the model.

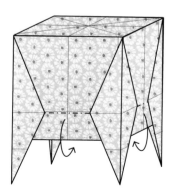

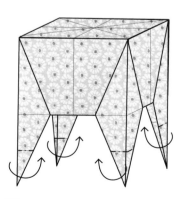

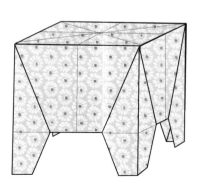

**11** Fold the lower edges inside on all four sides.

**12** Fold the points into the model along the creases made previously in step 5.

**13** Complete.

# BEDSIDE LAMP

**The bedside lamps are made in the same way as the standard lamp on page 32. The height of the lamp stand has been reduced to create a table lamp by using a square instead of a rectangle for the base.**

For the bedside lamp, follow the instructions on page 32. For each lamp, use a $2^{15}/_{16}$ x $2^{15}/_{16}$in square for the base and a $4^{5}/_{16}$ x $2^{3}/_{16}$in rectangle for the shade.

# DRESSING TABLE

**The dressing table is the same model as the base of the hutch on page 76, without the shelves. The mirror is a scaled-down version of the full-length mirror shown overleaf.**

For the dressing table, follow the instructions on page 76, using a $6^{7}/_{8}$ x $6^{7}/_{8}$in square.

For the dressing-table mirror, follow the instructions on page 108, using a $2^{3}/_{4}$ x $2^{3}/_{4}$in square.

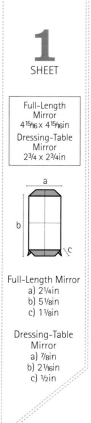

Full-Length
Mirror
4¹⁵/₁₆ x 4¹⁵/₁₆in
Dressing-Table
Mirror
2³/₄ x 2³/₄in

Full-Length Mirror
a) 2¹/₄in
b) 5¹/₈in
c) 1¹/₈in

Dressing-Table
Mirror
a) ⁷/₈in
b) 2¹/₁₆in
c) ¹/₂in

# MIRROR

**The mirror can be made in different sizes, to stand either on the floor or on a table (see page 107). The model is made from a square, but it is possible to change its length by adjusting the dimensions of the starting sheet.**

Follow these instructions for the dressing-table mirror on page 107.

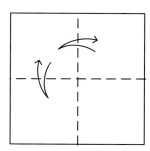

**1** Start with a square, colored side down. Fold and unfold it in half lengthwise along both axes.

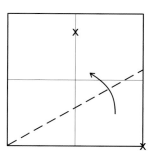

**2** Fold the lower left corner up diagonally. The fold should start from the opposite corner and cause the corner (x) to touch the center crease (x).

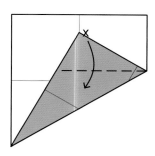

**3** Fold the corner back down so that the upper edge aligns with the folded edge beneath.

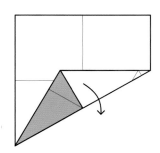

**4** Unfold back to a square.

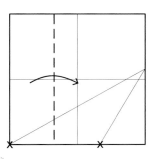

**5** Fold the edge in to touch the crease made in step 3.

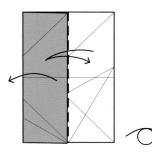

**6** Fold and unfold the opposite edge over. Then unfold the model and turn it over.

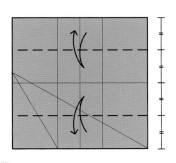

**7** Fold and unfold the upper and lower edges to the middle crease.

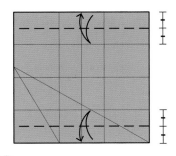

**8** Fold and unfold the edges to the creases made previously.

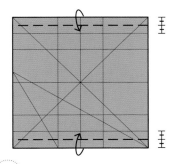

**9** Fold the edges to the creases made previously.

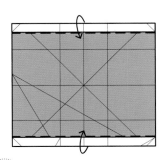

**10** Fold the edges over again.

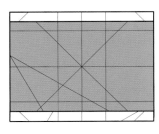

**11** Turn the model over.

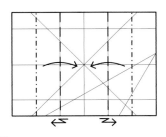

**12** Fold the sides in and out again where indicated.

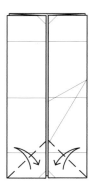

**13** Fold and unfold the lower corners.

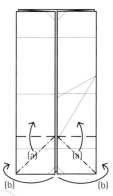

**14** Fold the lower edges up (a). Then open and flatten the corners (b).

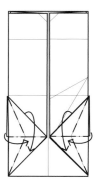

**15** Fold the corners down. At the same time, fold in the edges of the triangular sections.

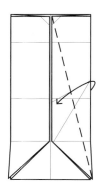

**16** Fold the right edge in diagonally.

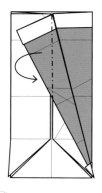

**17** Fold the corner of the folded section behind.

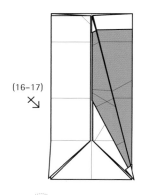

(16–17)

**18** Repeat steps 16–17 on the other side.

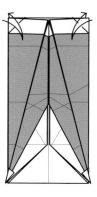

**19** Fold and unfold the upper corners.

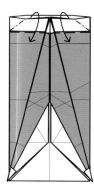

**20** Fold the upper layer of the upper edge down. This will cause the outer corners to fold in.

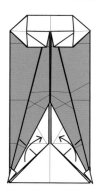

**21** Fold the lower points up.

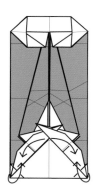

**22** Fold the lower corners up. Then fold the points back down.

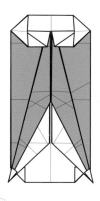

**23** Turn the model over.

**24** Complete.

6⅞
x
6⅞ in

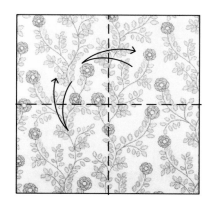

a) 1¾in
b) 3½in
c) 1¾in

# SLIPPER CHAIR

**The slipper-style chair has a fuller rounded back that gives it a feminine feel. This chair can be made in alternative patterns or colors and used in any of the room sets.**

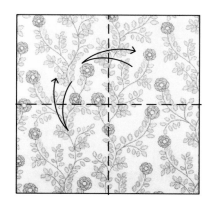

**1**   Start with a square, colored side up. Fold and unfold it in half lengthwise along both axes.

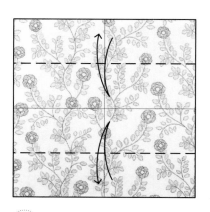

**2**   Fold and unfold the upper and lower edges to the middle.

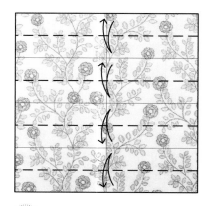

**3**   Fold and unfold between the creases made previously. This will divide the paper into eight equal sections.

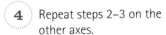

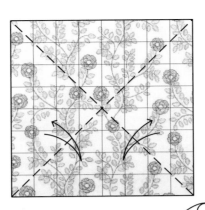

**4** Repeat steps 2–3 on the other axes.

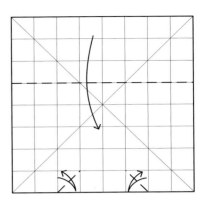

**5** Fold and unfold the square diagonally along both axes. Then turn the model over.

**6** Fold and unfold the small diagonal folds at the lower edge where indicated. Then fold the upper section down at the three-eighths crease.

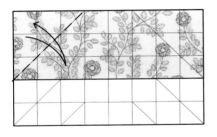

**7** Fold and unfold the upper left corner.

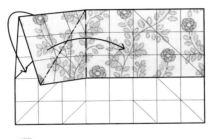

**8** Fold the corner over, reverse the fold made previously and flatten.

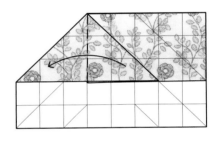

**9** Fold the corner back again.

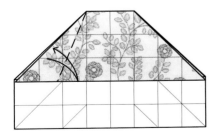

**10** Fold and unfold the diagonal folded edge to the adjacent crease.

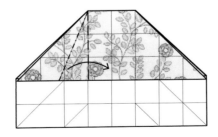

**11** Fold the corner up, open the layers of the point, and flatten.

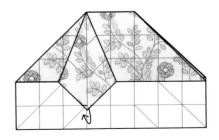

**12** Fold the tip of the flattened point behind. This fold should be aligned with the crease in the layer below.

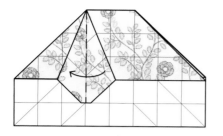

**13** Fold one side over.

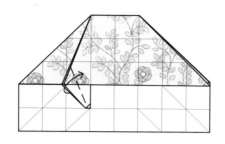

**14** Fold the edge in to cause the edge to touch the adjacent crease.

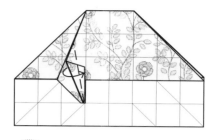

**15** Fold the edge in again.

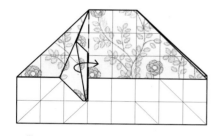

**16** Fold the edge over.

(13–16)

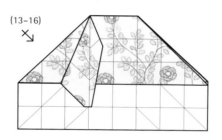

**17** Repeat steps 13–16 on the other side of the point.

(10–17)

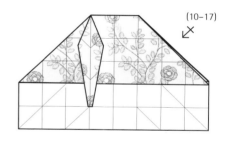

**18** Repeat steps 10–17 on the right side.

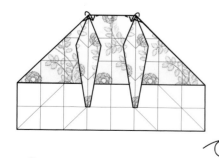

**19** Fold over the outer corners of the upper edge. Then turn the model over.

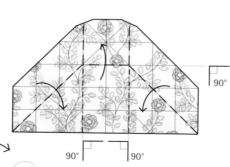

**20** Fold the outer edges in, causing the middle section to fold up. Note: The right-angle symbols show perpendicular folds.

**21** This shows the fold described in step 20 in progress.

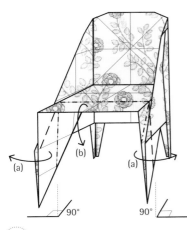

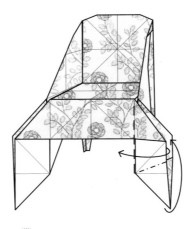

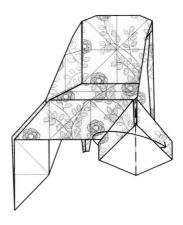

**22** Fold the two sides (a) out to be perpendicular to the sides of the model. The front edge (b) will fold down.

**23** Fold the front layer of one side over. This will cause the point to open and fold up.

**24** Fold one side over to see the reverse.

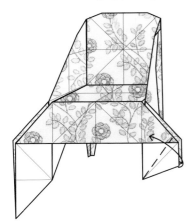

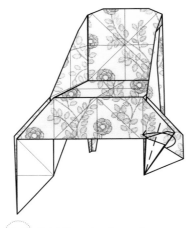

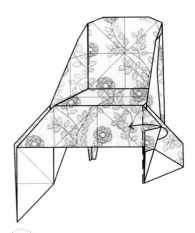

**25** Fold the front layer of the leg in.

**26** Fold the edge in again, narrowing the leg.

**27** Fold the front layer over to lie flat with the edge of the seat.

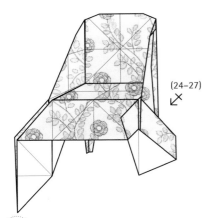

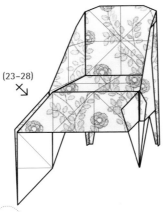

**28** Repeat steps 24–27 on the other side of leg.

**29** Repeat steps 23–28 on the other side of the chair.

**30** Complete.

# BATHROOM

No house would be complete without a bathroom. Here we have a classic suite comprising a toilet, sink, and bathtub. Made in white, the toilet and sink look like traditional white porcelain, a neutral color that is popular throughout the world. The sides of the freestanding bathtub are a smart dark gray, which looks fresh and contemporary, but you could create a kitsch effect with different colors or by adding a seat cover to the toilet.

WALLS Graham & Brown, Floral Sketch, Red and Pink, 50-553
FLOOR Graham & Brown, Cavern, Green, 32-242

# BATHTUB

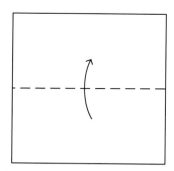

6⁷⁄₈
x
6⁷⁄₈in

a) 5in
b) 1³⁄₄in
c) 2in

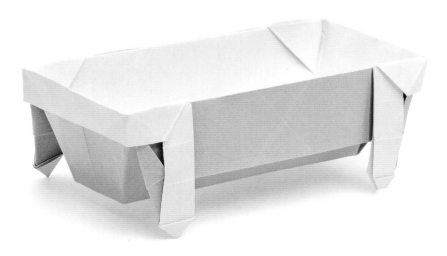

This model represents a classic roll-top bath.
The feet are made from the corners of the square while the
middle of the paper is shaped to become the rounded tub
shape. The penultimate step of the folding sequence
is particularly satisfying as it locks the model
together and gives it rigidity.

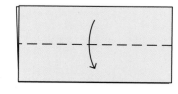

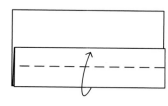

**1** Start with a square, colored side down, and fold it in half widthwise.

**2** Fold the upper edge down to the lower folded edge.

**3** Fold the lower edge up to the folded edge above.

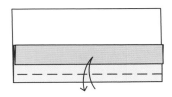

**4** Fold up the lower edge to touch the folded edge above, then unfold it.

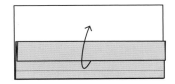

**5** Unfold the upper folded edge.

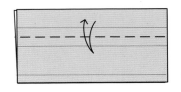

**6** Fold and unfold between the creases. Then turn the model over.

(2–6)

**7** Repeat steps 2–6.

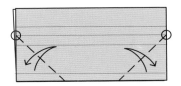

**8** Fold and unfold the lower corners up to the crease indicated.

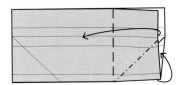

**9** Fold the upper right layer over. Then open and squash the outer corner.

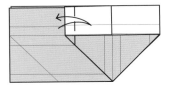

**10** Fold and unfold the edge along the crease in the upper layer.

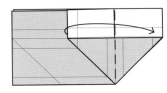

**11** Fold the section back.

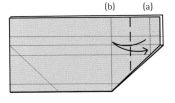

(b)   (a)

**12** Fold and unfold the edge over to align the crease (a) with the crease (b).

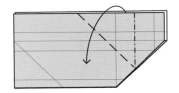

**13** Fold the upper corner down and open out the layer underneath.

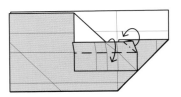

**14** Fold the edge down. This will cause the outer corner to squash flat.

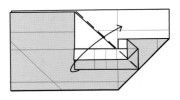

**15** Fold the corner back up. Do not unfold the corner from step 14

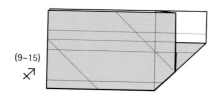

(9–15)

**16** Repeat steps 9–15 on the other side.

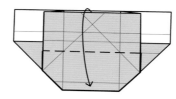

**17** Fold the upper layer down.

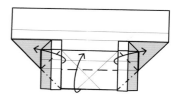

**18** Fold the sides of the section out to the left and right, and fold the lower edge up.

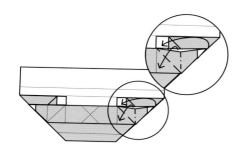

**19** Fold the corner up, separate the layers, and flatten.

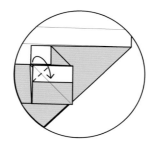

**20** Fold the tip over.

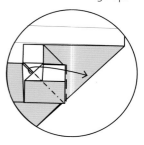

**21** Fold the section back to a point.

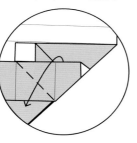

**22** Fold the corner down along the crease indicated.

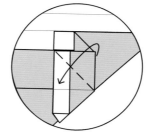

**23** Fold the corner of the section down.

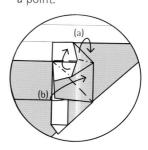

**24** Fold the upper squashed corner back (a). This will cause the corner (b) to fold back.

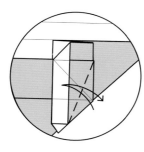

**25** Fold and unfold between the upper crease and the corner of the folded tip.

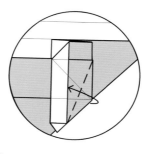

**26** Fold the corner in and underneath the adjacent folded edge.

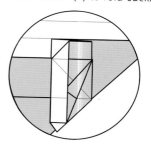

**27** Leg complete.

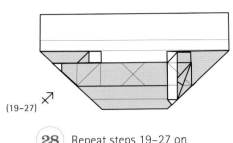

(19-27)

**28** Repeat steps 19–27 on the other side.

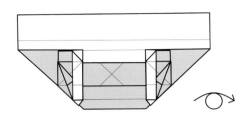

**29** Turn the model over.

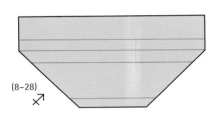

(8-28)

**30** Repeat steps 8–28.

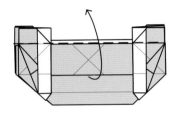

**31** Fold the lower edge up.

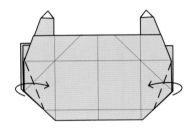

**32** Fold the corners in between the creases indicated.

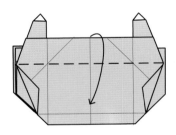

**33** Fold the upper edge down.

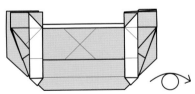

**34** Turn the model over.

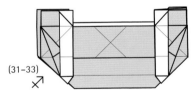

(31-33)

**35** Repeat steps 31–33.

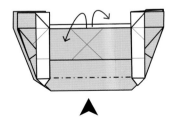

**36** Open out the model and re-form the crease to shape the tub.

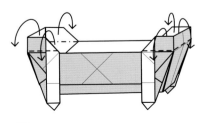

**37** Fold the edge over at each end to lock the folds beneath.

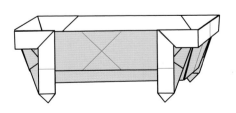

**38** Complete.

# SINK

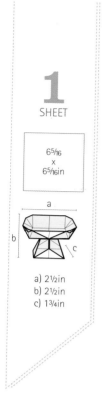

6⁵⁄₁₆
x
6⁵⁄₁₆in

a

b

c

a) 2½in
b) 2½in
c) 1³⁄₄in

This model combines several folding techniques.
The bowl of the sink is folded to form a round shape that
is held in place by folded corners. The pedestal is folded
flat and then opened up to make a three-dimensional base.
As is the case with the other models shown made from
white paper, the upper side is shaded in the
folding diagrams below.

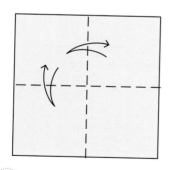

**1** Start with a square, colored
side up. Fold and unfold it
in half lengthwise along
both axes.

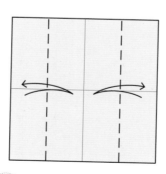

**2** Fold and unfold both sides
to the middle.

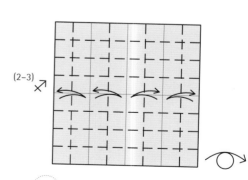

(2–3)

**3** Fold and unfold between the
creases to divide the square
into eight equal sections. Then
repeat steps 2–3 on the other
axis and turn the model over.

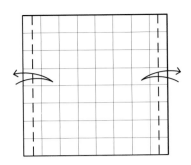

**4** Fold and unfold lengthwise between the edges and the adjacent creases on both sides.

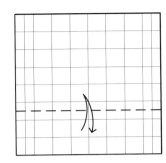

**5** Fold and unfold the lower edge between the second and third creases.

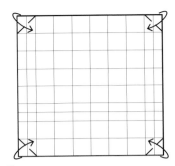

**6** Fold in the corners to align the edges with the one-eighth crease.

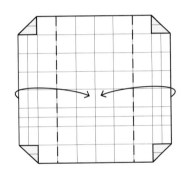

**7** Fold both sides in to the middle crease.

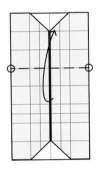

**8** Fold the lower section up along the five-eighths crease.

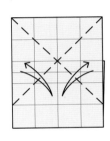

**9** Fold and unfold the upper corners diagonally.

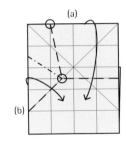

**10** Fold the upper edge (a) down and refold the left diagonal (b). Note the reference points of the second diagonal fold.

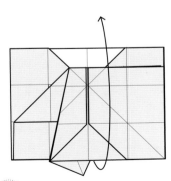

**11** Unfold the model back to step 10.

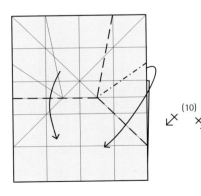

**12** Repeat step 10 on the other side.

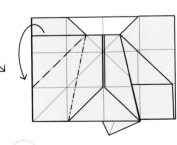

**13** Refold the creases from step 10 on the left side.

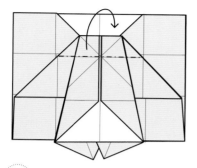

**14** Fold the upper edge of the front folded section behind.

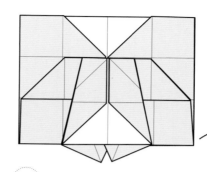

**15** Turn the model over.

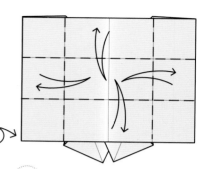

**16** Fold and unfold all four edges in along the creases made previously.

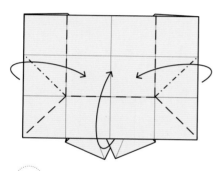

**17** Fold the outer and lower edges in together.

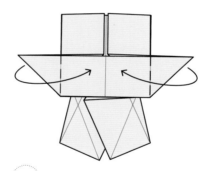

**18** Fold the outer corners in.

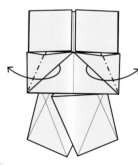

**19** Fold the points up to be perpendicular to the base, separate the layers, and flatten them.

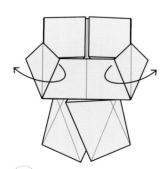

**20** Unfold to step 16.

(17–19)

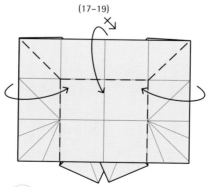

**21** Repeat steps 17–19 on the upper edge.

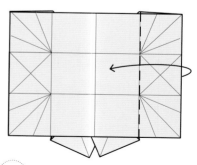

**22** Fold the right side in.

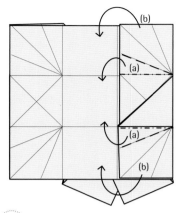

**23** Slide the upper and lower right corners (a) beneath the middle section. This will cause the corners (b) to fold in.

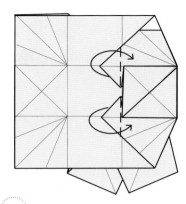

**24** Fold the corners over.

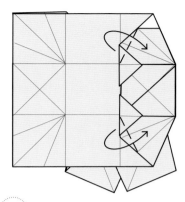

**25** Fold the outer corners over again.

(22–25)

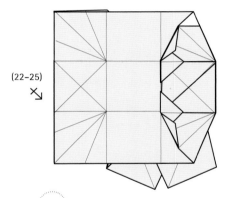

**26** Repeat steps 22–25 on the left side.

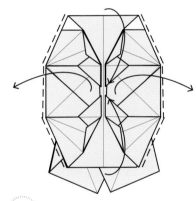

**27** Fold out the folded edges, causing the upper and lower edges to fold in. Then shape the bowl.

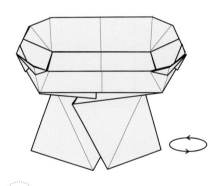

**28** Rotate the model to look at the reverse side.

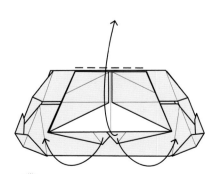

**29** Fold the pedestal section up, and open out the paper beneath.

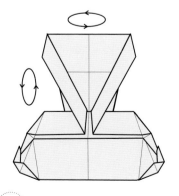

**30** Turn the model over and rotate it.

**31** Complete.

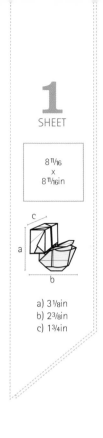

**1 SHEET**

8 ¹¹/₁₆
x
8 ¹¹/₁₆in

a) 3 ¹/₈in
b) 2 ³/₈in
c) 1 ³/₄in

# TOILET

As with the sink, the toilet combines different folding techniques. Rounder folds are used for the bowl and more angular conventional folds for the tank.

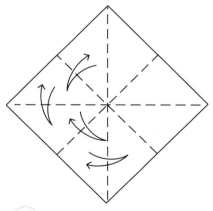

( **1** ) Start with a square, colored side down. Fold and unfold it in half lengthwise and diagonally along both axes.

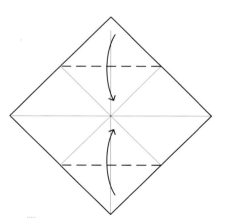

( **2** ) Fold the upper and lower corners to the middle.

( **3** ) Turn the model over.

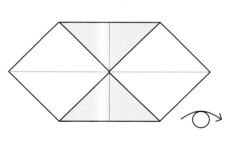

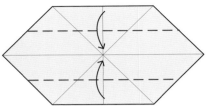

**4** Fold the upper and lower edges to the middle.

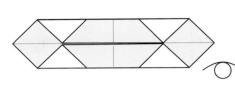

**5** Turn the model over.

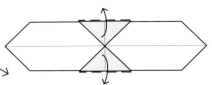

**6** Fold the corners out.

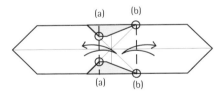

**7** Fold the corners in to the folded edge.

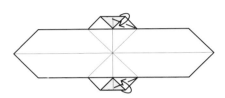

**8** Fold the outer right edges in to touch the folded edge.

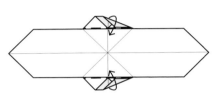

**9** Fold the upper and lower sections in and over the folded edge.

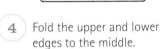
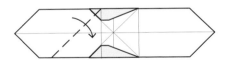

**10** Fold and unfold the left side of the model, parallel to the folded corners in the upper layer (a). Fold and unfold the right side where indicated, at the tips of the folded sections (b).

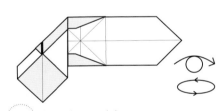

**11** Fold the left section over diagonally. The upper edge should align with the adjacent crease.

**12** Turn the model over, left to right.

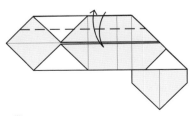

**13** Fold and unfold the upper edge to the middle crease.

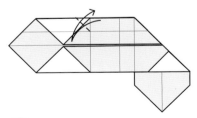

**14** Fold and unfold the diagonal indicated at the upper edge.

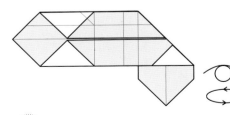

**15** Turn the model over, left to right.

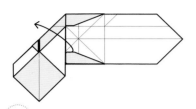

**16** Fold the section back up.

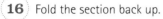
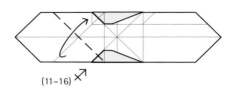

(11–16)

**17** Repeat steps 11–16 on the lower section.

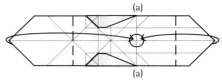

(a)

(a)

**18** Fold the sides in. The corners should touch at the crease indicated (a)–(a).

**19** Fold the sides back out.

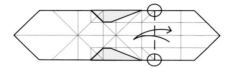

**20** Fold and unfold the right side. Fold at the point where the diagonal fold touches the edge.

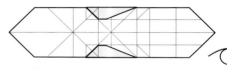

**21** Turn the model over, left to right.

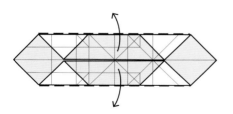

**22** Fold the upper and lower edges out.

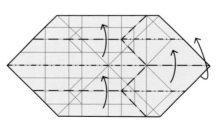

**23** Refold the model. At the same time, reverse-fold up the right side.

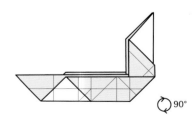

90°

**24** Rotate the model 90° clockwise.

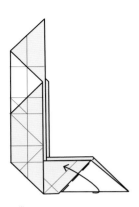

**25** Fold the lower right corner up.

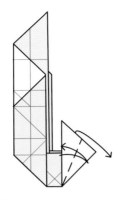

**26** Fold and unfold the corner back to the folded edge. Unfold the section.

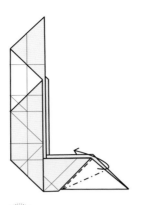

**27** Reverse the corner into the model.

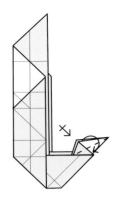

**28** Fold the edges over in front and behind.

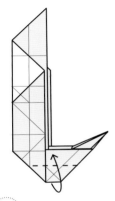

**29** Fold the upper layer of the lower edge up.

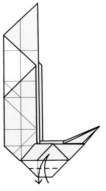

**30** Fold and unfold the lower edge.

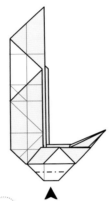

**31** Reverse the lower edge inside the model.

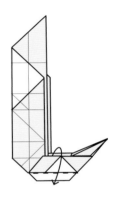

**32** Fold the edge down again.

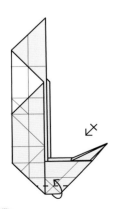

**33** Fold the lower edge up to align with the crease above. Repeat behind.

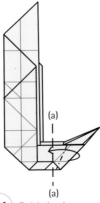

**34** Fold the lower corner up along (a)–(a). Then separate the layers and flatten.

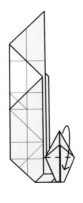

**35** Fold the point down.

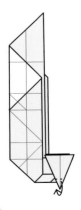

**36** Fold the tip of the point behind.

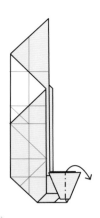

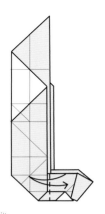

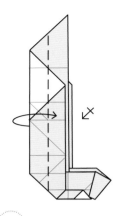

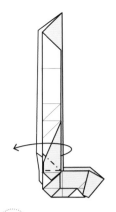

**37** Fold out the section.

**38** Fold and unfold where indicated.

**39** Fold the left edge over to touch the edge on the other side.

**40** Reverse-fold the point down to the left. When doing this, open it out and flatten.

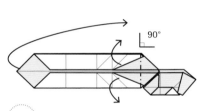

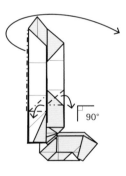

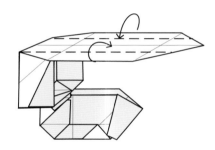

**41** Fold the point back up. Open it up and fold out the edges.

**42** Fold the upper section to the right. At the same time, fold out the edges.

**43** Fold the edges of the upper section into the middle.

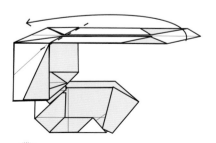

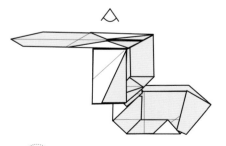

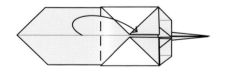

**44** Fold the section over, along the edge of the tank.

**45** The next step will look at the model from above.

**46** Fold the section over, left to right.

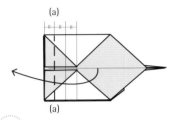

**47** Fold the point back where indicated (a)–(a).

**48** Fold the edges of the outer section in. This will cause the corners to fold over and squash.

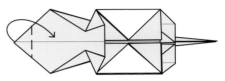

**49** Fold the tip over.

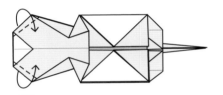

**50** Fold the edges in.

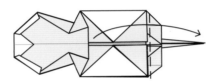

**51** Fold the whole section back.

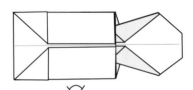

**52** The next step will show a side view.

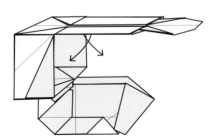

**53** Fold the inner folded edges of the upper section down.

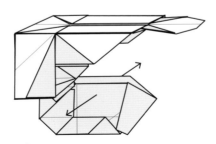

**54** Open out and shape the bowl.

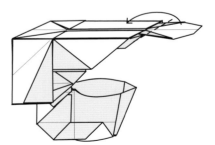

**55** Fold the end of the upper section over.

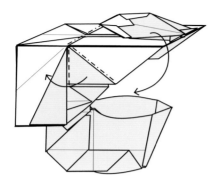

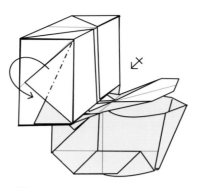

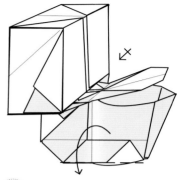

**56** Fold the upper section down. At the same time, open out the paper beneath and fold it around the tank.

**57** Fold the outer corner into the pocket formed in the layer beneath. This should lock the edge of the tank together. Repeat on the other side.

**58** Fold the lower edge down to form a base. Repeat on the other side.

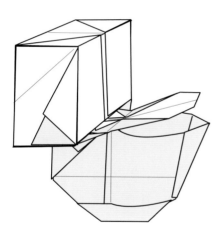

**59** Complete.

# MIRROR

The mirror featured in the bathroom is the same as the full-length mirror in the bedroom (see page 108), showing how interchangeable the models are. Alternatively, make a chair to match your bathroom scheme if you prefer.

For the mirror, follow the instructions on page 108, using a 4$^{15}$/$_{16}$ x 4$^{15}$/$_{16}$in square.

# RUG

The graphic floral pattern of the wallpaper used to decorate the bathroom set lent itself particularly well to creating a circular rug, simply by cutting around the outline of a motif.

The diameter of the rug is approximately 4$^{3}$/$_{4}$in. Use wallpaper or an offcut of origami paper.

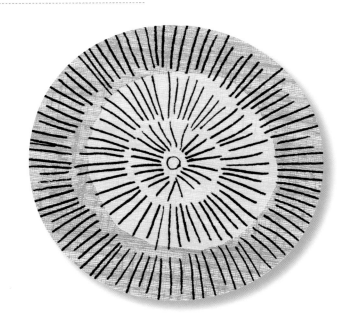

# FOOTSTOOL

The model for the bedside table on page 105 has been made up in a star-patterned paper to create a handy footstool in a colorway that coordinates with the bathroom design.

To make the footstool, follow the instructions for the bedside table on page 105, using a 4$^{5}$/$_{16}$ x 4$^{5}$/$_{16}$in square.

# TERRACE

Relax outside on sunloungers patterned with a lush rainforest design. The terrace space is bordered by "plants," with the walls covered with mixed foliage and bamboo. A trio of terracotta plant pots breaks up the space, with elegant tall flowers that add splashes of bright color. The predominant hue is green, which gives the space a verdant, fresh atmosphere, but other colors and patterns could be introduced by using different papers for the sunloungers and pots.

**WALLS** Osborne & Little, Nina Campbell Wallpaper Album 3, Arboretum, NCW4022-02 (left), and Farrow & Ball, Bamboo, BP2139 (right)
**FLOOR** Osborne & Little, Teatro Wallpaper, Quadrato, W6038-01

6⁷/₈
x
6⁷/₈in

a) 1³/₄in
b) 1¹/₂in
c) 4⁵/₈in

# SUNLOUNGER

This model uses triangular folds to create legs that stand perpendicular to the seat. The folding process gives the model its rigidity with some three-dimensional folding techniques. Add a throw pillow in a complementary color to finish the project.

For the throw pillow, follow the instructions on page 24, using a 3⁷/₁₆ x 3⁷/₁₆in square.

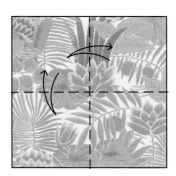

**1** Start with a square, colored side up. Fold and unfold it in half lengthwise along both axes.

**2** Fold and unfold the upper and lower edges to the middle.

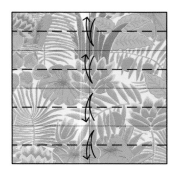

**3** Fold and unfold between the creases made previously. This will divide the paper into eight equal sections.

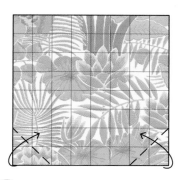

(2-3)

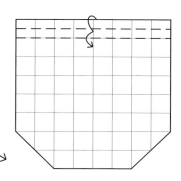

**4** Repeat steps 2–3 on the other axis.

**5** Fold the two lower corners in where indicated. Then turn the model over.

**6** Fold the upper edge over to the crease below. Then fold it over again.

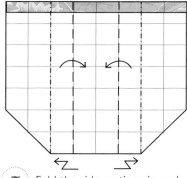

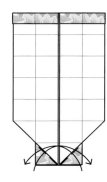

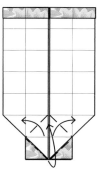

**7** Fold the side sections in and out again where indicated.

**8** Fold and unfold the lower corners.

**9** Fold the lower edge up. At the same time, open it up and flatten.

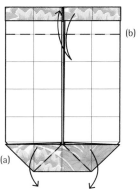

(b)

(a)

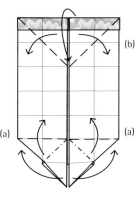

(b)

(a)              (a)

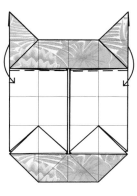

**10** On the lower section (a), fold down the corners. Fold and unfold the upper edge (b).

**11** Fold up the lower section at (a)–(a) and open the section. Fold out the upper corners and flatten (b). This refolds the crease from step 10 (b).

**12** Reverse-fold the upper corners inside the model.

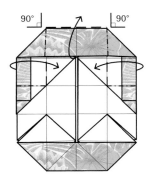

90° | 90°

**13** Fold the edges of the upper section in to stand up and be perpendicular to the base.

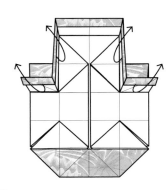

**14** Fold out one of the folded layers.

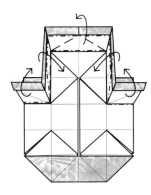

**15** Fold the edges together and flatten the upper section.

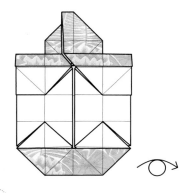

**16** Turn the model over.

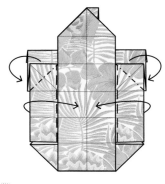

**17** Fold the upper layer of the sides in, squashing the upper corners.

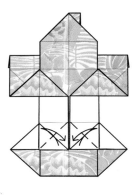

**18** Fold and unfold the corners of the lower section.

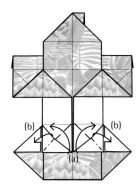

**19** Fold the corners up at (a), and fold the upper layer out (b).

**20** Fold the inner layers over.

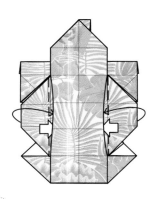

**21** Fold the edges in and tuck them into the adjacent pockets.

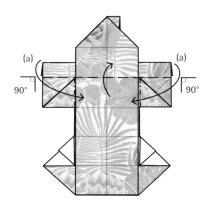

**22** Fold the lower section up. At the same time, fold in the two sides (a).

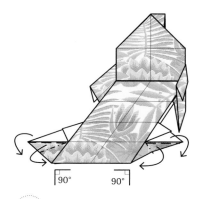

**23** Fold the front corner triangles (patterned) together. This will cause the paper behind (white) to fold down.

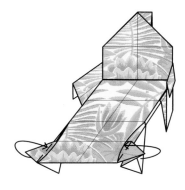

**24** Fold the triangles up into the adjacent pockets.

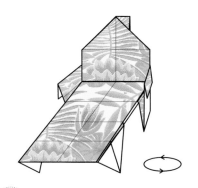

**25** Rotate the model to work on the reverse.

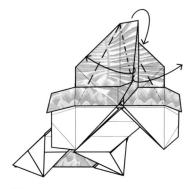

**26** Open out the rear section and fold it flat.

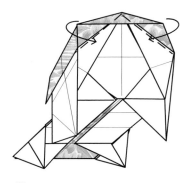

**27** Fold the edges over.

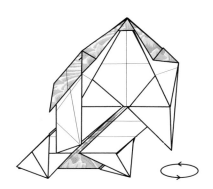

**28** Rotate the model to work on the front.

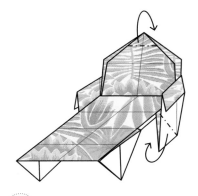

**29** Fold the corners of the legs behind on both sides. Then fold the tip of the upper section behind.

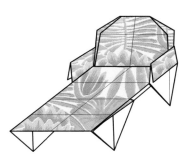

**30** Complete.

# PLANT POT

Small Pot
3⁷⁄₁₆ x 3⁷⁄₁₆in

Large Pot
6⁷⁄₈ x 6⁷⁄₈in

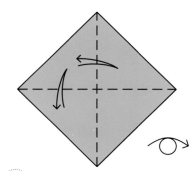

a

b

c

Small Pot
a) ¹⁵⁄₁₆in
b) 1⅛in
c) ¹⁵⁄₁₆in

Large Pot
a) 1¹⁵⁄₁₆in
b) 2¼in
c) 1¹⁵⁄₁₆in

**The plant pot or vase can be made as a stand-alone piece or together with the flowers on page 143. The smaller pot holds a single stem, while the larger pot can hold up to three flowers.**

The folding instructions are the same for both sizes of pot.

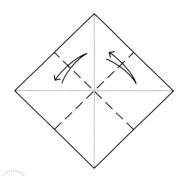

**1** Start with a square, colored side up. Fold and unfold it in half diagonally along both axes. Then turn the model over.

**2** Fold and unfold in half lengthwise along both axes.

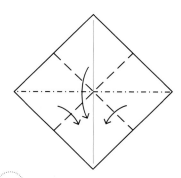

**3** Refold the creases from steps 1 and 2 simultaneously. This will make all of the corners touch. The fold is sometimes called a preliminary base.

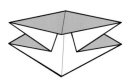

**4** Fold in progress.

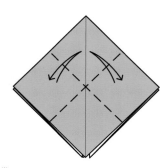

**5** Fold and unfold the model in half lengthwise through all layers along both axes.

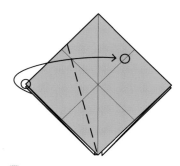

**6** Fold the left corner in to touch the crease made in step 5. The fold should start at the lower corner.

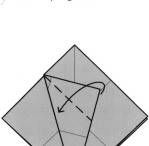

**7** Fold the corner down to touch the folded edge.

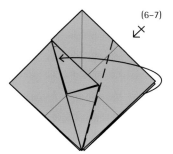

(6–7)

**8** Repeat steps 6–7 on the other side.

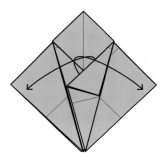

**9** Unfold the folded edges.

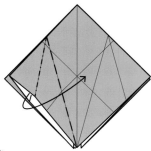

**10** Fold the left side over, open the layers, and squash the point flat.

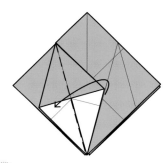

**11** Fold the layer back over.

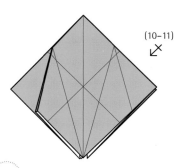

(10–11)

**12** Repeat steps 10–11 on the other side.

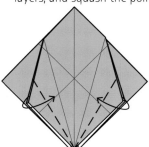

**13** Fold the outer edges in to the creases on both sides.

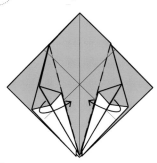

**14** Fold the outer edges in again.

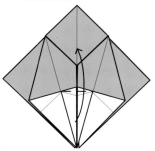

**15** Fold the lower point up.

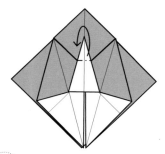

**16** Fold the tip of the point behind and into the model.

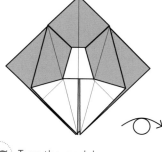

**17** Turn the model over.

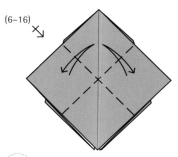

(6–16)

**18** Repeat steps 6–16 on the reverse.

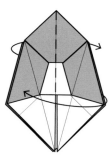

**19** Fold over one layer at the front and one behind to expose the hidden sides.

(13–16)

**20** Repeat steps 13–16 on the front and behind.

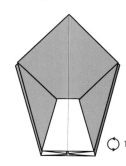

180°

**21** Rotate the model 180°.

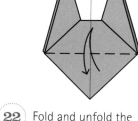

**22** Fold and unfold the lower corner.

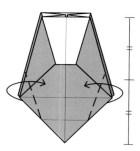

**23** Fold and unfold between the lower corner and the crease made previously.

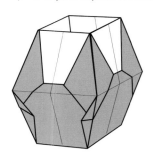

**24** Fold the edges in. The fold should start from the crease made in step 23 to just beyond halfway.

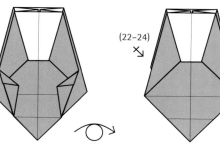

**25** Turn the model over.

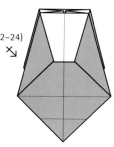

(22–24)

**26** Repeat steps 22–24 in front and behind.

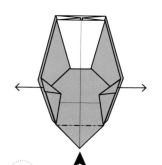

**27** Open up the model and shape the pot.

**28** Complete.

# FLOWER

## 2
SHEETS

| Flower Head |
| --- |
| 1³/₄ x 1³/₄in |

| Stem |
| --- |
| 3⁷/₁₆ x 3⁷/₁₆in |

a) 3³/₄in
b) ¹¹/₁₆in
c) ¹¹/₁₆in

The flower is a two-piece model. One square is used for the flower head and another for the stem. The flower head should be made from a square with sides half as long as the square used to make the stem. If the stem and pot are made from squares of the same size, the flower will fit in the pot.

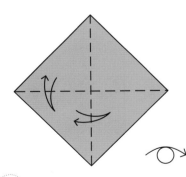

**1** Start with a square, colored side up. Fold and unfold it in half diagonally along both axes. Then turn it over.

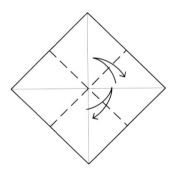

**2** Fold and unfold the square in half lengthwise along both axes.

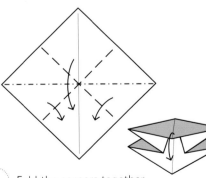

**3** Fold the corners together and fold the edges in along the folds made previously. This is sometimes called a preliminary base.

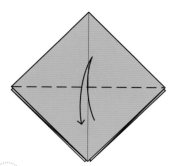

**4** Fold and unfold along the middle.

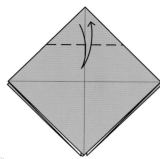

**5** Fold and unfold between the upper corner and the crease made previously.

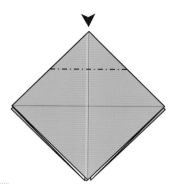

**6** Reverse-fold the corner into the model. (Step 7 shows this in progress.)

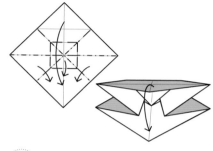

**7** Reverse-fold in progress. The process opens the model back to a square and reverse-folds the middle inside along the creases made in step 5.

**8** Rotate the model 180°.

○ 180°

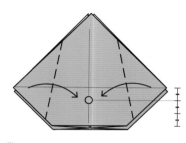

**9** Fold the sides in. The outer corners should touch a point about one-third of the way between the crease and the lower edge.

**10** Fold the lower right corner in.

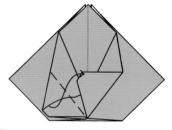

**11** Fold the lower left corner over and tuck the right folded corner into the pocket on the left.

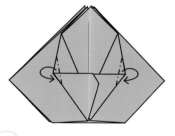

**12** Fold the edges behind.

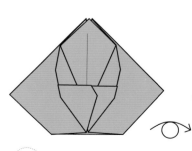

**13** Turn the model over.

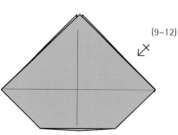

(9–12)

**14** Repeat steps 9–12.

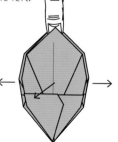

**15** Open out the flower.

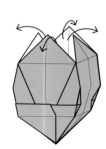

**16** Complete.

# STEM

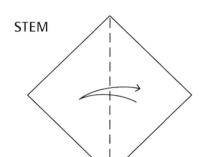 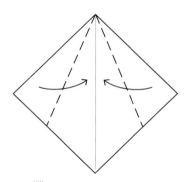 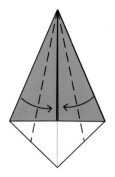

**1** Start with a square, colored side down. Fold and unfold it in half diagonally.

**2** Fold the sides in to the middle crease.

**3** Fold the edges in again to the middle crease.

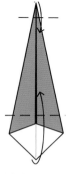 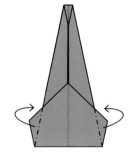 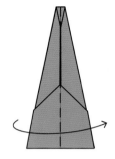 

**4** Fold the upper tip down and the lower corner (white) up.

**5** Fold the corners behind on both sides.

**6** Fold the model in half lengthwise.

**7** Stem complete.

## PUTTING THE FLOWER, STEM, AND PLANT POT TOGETHER

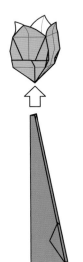 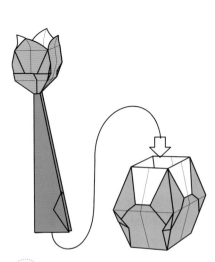 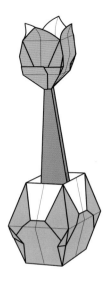

**1** Insert the stem into the base of the flower head.

**2** Insert the base of the stem into the pot.

**3** Complete.

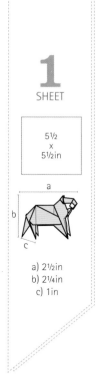

5½
x
5½in

a

b

c

a) 2½in
b) 2¼in
c) 1in

# PET

No house would be complete without a pet. This model is a little ambiguous, as some see it as a cat and others as a dog. So whether you are firmly in the feline or canine camp, here is a chance to make a playful companion to add to your paper household. The pet is at home in any room, but do keep it off the sofa.

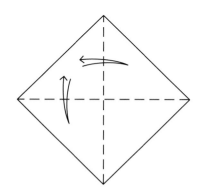

**1** Start with a square, colored side down. Fold and unfold it in half diagonally along both axes.

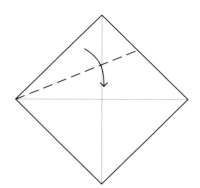

**2** Fold the upper left edge down and align it with the middle crease.

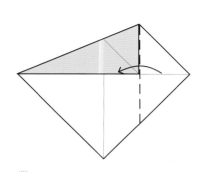

**3** Fold the right corner over.

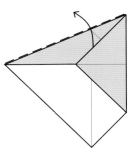

**4** Unfold the upper left edge folded in step 2.

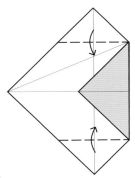

**5** Fold the upper and lower corners in at the corners of the folded triangle.

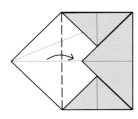

**6** Fold the left corner in at the edges of the folded triangles.

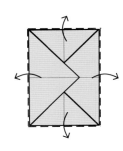

**7** Open out the model.

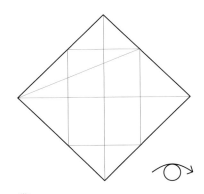

**8** Turn the model over.

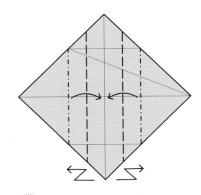

**9** Fold both sides in along the inner valley fold and then back again along the parallel valley fold where indicated.

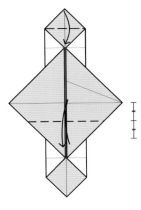

**10** Fold the top corner down, then fold and unfold the lower section where indicated.

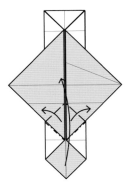

**11** Fold the lower section up, open out the upper edges, and fold it flat.

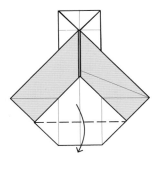

**12** Fold the corner back down again.

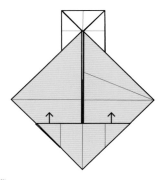

**13** Reverse-fold out the paper beneath the folded section.

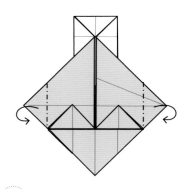

**14** Fold the corners at each side behind.

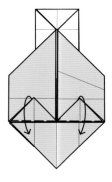

**15** Fold the points down.

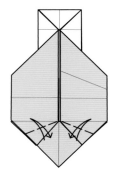

**16** Fold up and unfold the lower corners.

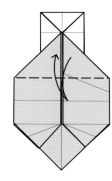

**17** Fold and unfold the upper section.

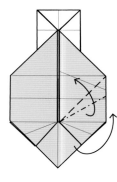

**18** Fold the upper layer up to the right. This will cause the lower folded triangle to fold up along the crease made in step 16.

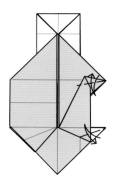

**19** Fold and unfold the edges.

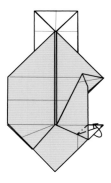

**20** Fold the lower edge back in and fold it under the upper layer.

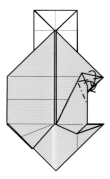

**21** Fold the upper edge over. At the same time, fold the adjacent inner edge into the model.

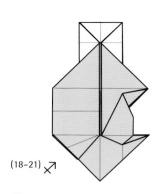

**22** Repeat steps 18–21 on the other side.

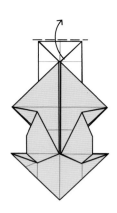

**23** Fold the upper corner up.

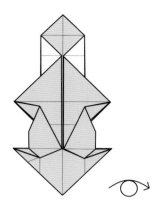

**24** Turn the model over.

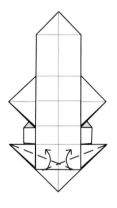

**25** Fold the lower corners in to the crease above (they will intersect).

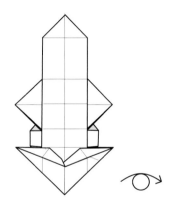

**26** Turn the model over.

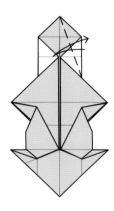

**27** Fold and unfold the upper right corner.

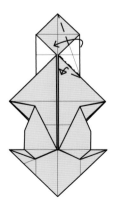

**28** Fold the edge back in. At the same time, fold the lower edge down.

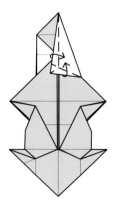

**29** Fold the edges back in.

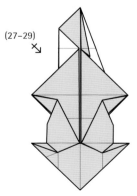

**30** Repeat steps 27–29 on the other side of the upper section.

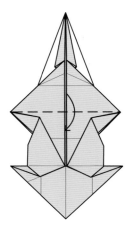

**31** Fold the upper section down.

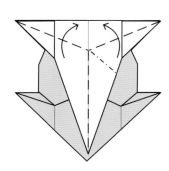

**32** Fold the lower edges of the upper section in. This will cause the point to narrow. Fold it to the right.

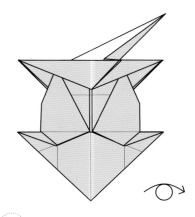

**33** Turn the model over.

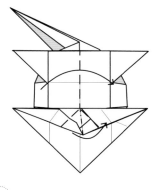

**34** Fold the left side over. At the same time, reverse the corner of the middle section.

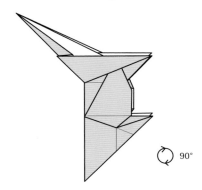

**35** Rotate the model 90° clockwise.

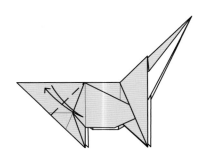

**36** Fold and unfold the left corner.

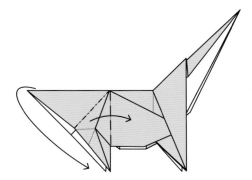

**37** Fold up the outer point, separate the layers, and flatten.

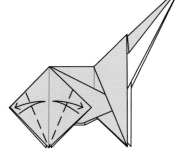

**38** Fold and unfold the lower edges to the middle crease.

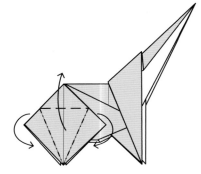

**39** Fold the upper layer up, in line with the ends of the creases made previously. This will cause the edges to fold in.

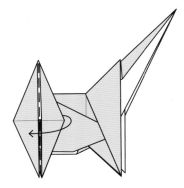

**40** Fold the edges of the rear section back together.

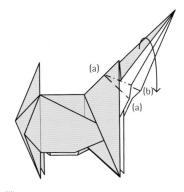

**41** Slide the point down. This will cause a valley fold at (a)–(a) on both sides. By making a mountain fold at (a)–(b) on both sides, the point will fold flat.

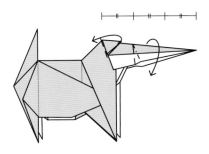

**42** Slide the point down again about two-thirds of the way along the point. (This repeats the folding process from step 41.)

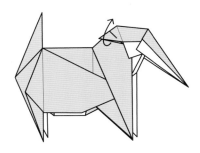

**43** Fold the corners of the section up to make ears on both sides.

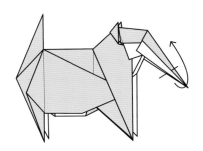

**44** Fold the tip of the point inside out to shorten it.

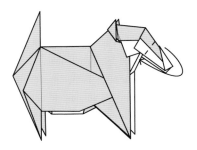

**45** Fold the section back inside the head.

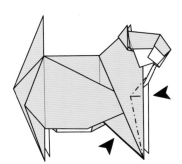

**46** Pinch both of the front legs to narrow them.

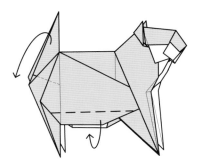

**47** Fold the lower edges in front and behind. Then fold the tail down.

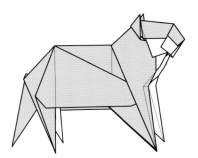

**48** Complete.

# RESOURCES AND ACKNOWLEDGMENTS

The following list includes paper-folding websites, paper suppliers, and details of some worldwide origami societies. If you wish to develop your interest further, most origami societies produce magazines, have their own publications, and organize meetings.

## AUTHOR'S WEBSITES
**Creaselightning (UK)**
www.creaselightning.co.uk
Mark Bolitho's website featuring his work.

**HP Origami printables (International)**
h30495.www3.hp.com/detail/1337.2
Weekly origami instructions produced by Creaselightning for Hewlett-Packard.

## ORIGAMI SOCIETIES
**Asociación Española de Papiroflexia**
www.pajarita.org
Spanish origami society.

**British Origami Society**
www.britishorigami.info
An established society with an international membership.

**Centro Diffusione Origami (CDO)**
www.origami-cdo.it
Italian origami society.

**European Origami Museum**
www.emoz.es
New origami museum in Zaragoza in northern Spain.

**Hungarian Origami Society**
www.ori-gami.hu

**Japan Origami Academic Society**
www.origami.gr.jp
Association with a good magazine on advanced folding techniques.

**Mouvement Français des Plieurs de Papier (MFPP)**
www.mfpp-origami.fr
French origami society.

**Nippon Origami Association**
www.origami-noa.jp
Japanese origami association with connections to an origami museum.

**Origami Deutschland**
www.papierfalten.de
German origami society.

**Origami Society of the Netherlands**
www.origami-osn.nl

**Origami USA**
www.origamiusa.org
With headquarters in New York, this society holds one of the biggest origami conventions of the year.

## OTHER RESOURCES
### USA AND CANADA

**Between the Folds**
www.greenfusefilms.com

A documentary featuring origami artists discussing their work and inspirations.

**Gilad's Origami Page**
www.giladorigami.com
Good selection of book reviews and origami information.

**The Japanese Paper Place**
www.japanesepaperplace.com
Origami supplies and Japanese paper.

**Kim's Crane**
www.kimscrane.com
Good supplier of paper and books.

**Origami L**
www.lists.digitalorigami.com
Discussion group on origami topics.

**Origami Sources**
www.origamisources.com
Information about origami, including a record of where origami has been used in films, television, and advertising.

**Origami Spirit**
www.origamispirit.com
Origami site with a blog and instructions.

**Origamido Studios**
www.origamido.com
A paper art studio, which also produces some of the best paper for origami.

### UK AND FRANCE

**Eric Joisel**
www.ericjoisel.com
The inspiring works of Eric Joisel.

**Jong ie Nara**
www.jongienara.co.uk
Good supplies of paper and products.

**The Origami Shop**
www.origami-shop.com
Good range of books and paper, including some self-published projects.

# PAPER CREDITS

## SET DECORATIONS
The author and publisher would like to thank the following companies for supplying wallpapers for set decoration: Farrow & Ball, Graham & Brown, Jane Churchill/Colefax and Fowler, Little Greene, Malabar, Mini Moderns, and Osborne & Little.

**LIVING ROOM**, page 14
**WALLS:** Jane Churchill, Brightwood Wallpapers, Willowbrook, Red/Blue, J140W-03. **FLOOR:** Little Greene, Heath Stripe, Cookie.

**MODERN-RETRO DINING ROOM**, page 36
**WALLS:** Mini Moderns, Festival Wallpaper, Concrete. **FLOOR:** Mini Moderns, Darjeeling Wallpaper, Welsh Slate.

**LOFT ROOM**, page 50
**WALLS:** Little Greene, Herbes, Cocktail (left), and Spring (right). **FLOOR:** Little Greene, Bark, Heath.

**FAMILY DINING ROOM**, page 64
**WALLS:** Farrow & Ball, Toile Trellis, BP620 (left), and BP669 (right). **FLOOR:** Farrow & Ball, Polka Square, BP1053.

**WORKSPACE**, page 82
**WALLS:** Mini Moderns, Vanessa Wallpaper, Mustard. **FLOOR:** Malabar, China Grass Wallpaper, Sisal Rice Wpsis01.

**BEDROOM**, page 98
**WALLS:** Farrow & Ball, Ocelot, BP3705 (left), and Wisteria, BP2217 (right). **FLOOR:** Farrow & Ball, Lattice, BP3502.

**BATHROOM**, page 116
**WALLS:** Graham & Brown, Floral Sketch, Red and Pink, 50-553. **FLOOR:** Graham & Brown, Cavern, Green, 32-242.

**TERRACE**, page 134
**WALLS:** Osborne & Little, Nina Campbell Wallpaper Album 3, Arboretum, NCW4022-02 (left), and Farrow & Ball, Bamboo, BP2139 (right). **FLOOR:** Osborne & Little, Teatro Wallpaper, Quadrato, W6038-01.

## PROJECTS AND PAPERS
The author and publisher would like to thank the following companies for their kind permission to reproduce wallpaper and fabric patterns on papers to create the projects in this book: Jane Churchill/Colefax and Fowler, Little Greene, Malabar, and Mini Moderns.

**Getting Started Easy Chair,** page 12: Jane Churchill, Mayflower, Doughnut (embroidery on cotton ground), Red/Blue, J658F-01.

**Living Room Cushioned Armchair, page 16:** Malabar, Fabric, Checks, Drum, Falkirk Check 10. **Two-Seater Sofa, page 22:** Jane Churchill, Alba, Calder (linen union), Green, J483F-02. **Throw Pillow, page 24:** Malabar, Fabric, Checks, Drum, Lennox Check 10. **Coffee Table, page 26:** Malabar, China Grass Wallpaper, Jute Ivory Wpjut01. **TV Stand, page 31:** Malabar, China Grass Wallpaper, Sisal Ecru Wpsis02. **Standard Lamp Lamp Shade, page 35:** Malabar, Fabric, Checks, Drum, Lennox Check 06.

**Modern-Retro Dining Room Octagonal Dining Table, page 38:** Mini Moderns, Backgammon Wallpaper, Mustard. **Picture in frame, page 48:** Mini Moderns, Festival Wallpaper, Bunting Blue and Red.

**Loft Room Deep-Cushioned Sofa, page 52:** Little Greene, Hepworth (wallpaper), Menthe. **Pillows, page 52 and Rug, page 63:** Malabar, Fabric, Stripes, Drum, Drum Stripe 02.

**Family Dining Room Rectangular Dining Table, page 66:** Jane Churchill, Mayflower, Doughnut (embroidery on cotton ground), Red/Blue, J658F-01. **Dining Chair, page 73:** Little Greene, St James's Place (wallpaper), Deep Blue.

**Workspace Desk, page 84:** Jane Churchill, Selworth Stripe, Dawlish Stripe (cotton fabric), Natural J670F-02. **Desk Chair, page 84:** Mini Moderns, Peggy Wallpaper, Lido. **Bookcase, page 90:** Malabar, China Grass Wallpaper, Jute Biscuit Wpjut05. **Armchair, page 93:** Jane Churchill, Brightwood, Vintage Daisy (cotton/linen fabric), Red/Green, J682F-03. **Armchair alternative colorway, page 97:** Malabar, Fabric, Stripes, Taka, Taka 01.

**Bedroom Bedcover, page 103:** Jane Churchill, Loren Autumn 2013, Fontane (fabric), Blue, J737F-02. **Bedside Table, page 105:** Jane Churchill, Albany, Lisette (fabric), Pale Blue, J674F-03. **Slipper Chair, page 112:** Jane Churchill, Fairhaven, Juliette (embroidery on fine linen ground), Blue, J579F-02.

**Bathroom Footstool, page 133:** Little Greene, Lower George St, Beryl.

**Terrace Sunlounger, page 136:** Little Greene, Reverie, Forest. **Throw Pillow, page 136:** Malabar, Fabric, Stripes, Taka, Taka 10.

## BOOK COVER
**FRONT COVER:** Living Room, page 14 (see left).
**BACK COVER, POCKET, AND INSIDE FRONT COVER:** Jane Churchill, Brightwood, Vintage Daisy (cotton/linen fabric), Red/Green, J682F-03.

## WALLPAPER SUPPLIERS
**Farrow & Ball**
www.farrow-ball.com
Tel: +44 (0)1202 876 141

**Graham & Brown**
www.grahambrown.com/uk
Tel: +44 (0)800 328 8452

**Jane Churchill at Colefax and Fowler**
www.janechurchill.com
Tel: +44 (0)20 8877 6400

**Little Greene**
www.littlegreene.com
Tel: +44 (0)845 880 5855

**Malabar**
www.malabar.co.uk
Tel: +44 (0)20 7501 4200

**Mini Moderns**
www.minimoderns.com

**Osborne & Little**
www.osborneandlittle.com
Tel: +44 (0)20 7352 1456